Navigating the Maze of Medicare

Other books by *Stephen J. Stellhorn*

Brokers, Financial Advisors & Insurance Agents
*An Investigative Process – the Book that **Some** May Not Want Their Clients to Read*

Available only in digital format for Kindle, Apple and Nook platforms

Navigating the Maze of Medicare – 2013 Edition
A Comprehensive Look at Your Coverage Choices

Available in softcover on Amazon.com

Navigating the Maze of Health Insurance Choices
A Comprehensive Look at Individual & Small Business Options

Available in softcover on Amazon.com
Available in digital format for Kindle, Apple and Nook platforms

Coming Soon on Amazon.com

Navigating the Maze of Social Security
Claiming Strategies for Fifty Shades of Grey

Navigating the Maze of Medicare

A Comprehensive Look at your Coverage Choices

2014 Edition

STEPHEN J. STELLHORN, RMA℠

CALMSEAS MEDIA
Tampa, Florida

Published by **CALMSEAS**MEDIA, Tampa, Florida

Cover design: Don Saunders
Photos: iStockphoto® and Photography by Robin.
Quotations: Courtesy *BrainyQuote*® unless otherwise noted.

Library of Congress Cataloging-in-Publication Data

Stellhorn, Stephen, 1954
    Navigating the Maze of Medicare: a comprehensive look at your coverage choices / Stephen Stellhorn.

        p. cm.
    Includes index.
    ISBN: 978-0-9894265-4-1
    CIP:

2014 Edition

Printed in the United States of America

Table of Contents

Request for Feedback vi

Acknowledgements... vii

Setting the Context ix

THE COST OF HEALTH CARE 1

THE MEDICARE PROGRAM... 21

MEDICARE TERMINOLOGY.. 49

ENROLLMENT & DISENROLLMENT PERIODS............................ 55

ORIGINAL MEDICARE PART A....................................... 79

ORIGINAL MEDICARE PART B....................................... 93

MEDICARE ADVANTAGE PART C PLANS............................ 105

MEDICARE PRESCRIPTION DRUG PART D PLANS 123

MEDICARE SUPPLEMENT/MEDIGAP PLANS........................... 143

CHOICES FOR LONG-TERM CARE 163

THE MEDICAID PROGRAM 213

WHAT YOU NEED TO KNOW BEFORE YOU BUY...................... 227

PLANNING THE MEDICARE BUYING DECISION........................ 235

ADDITIONAL MEDICARE RESOURCES................................. 247

About the Author 255

Index... 257

Request for Feedback

I am very respectful of your time and privacy. I will not share any information you provide without your expressed consent to do so. I also want to thank you in advance for your consideration.

I invite readers to share their feedback with me on this subject matter. What topics did I cover too much? Which should I have elaborated on more? Did I not include a topic that should have been covered with this subject matter? Should I have completely deleted a topic? Are there any mistakes such as typos, grammatical errors, etc. which I didn't catch?

Your comments are very valuable in helping to make future updates better. I've established an email address for receiving your feedback: readercommunity@msmcapital.net. Please insert the title of the book, "**Navigating the Maze of Medicare 2014**" in the subject line of your email.

Acknowledgements

I'd like to acknowledge the Aspiring Writers Marketing & Publishing Meetup group located in Tampa, Florida and especially Jewel Parago. From the first meeting I attended, to all the subsequent meetings, I have learned so much. The list of presenters who have come and shared their time and knowledge has been phenomenal. It has been a wonderful experience.

"Live your life and forget your age."

Dr. Norman Vincent Peale
Author, Professional Speaker and Minister

Setting the Context

"Together Wendy we can live with the sadness
I'll love you with all the madness in my soul
h-Oh, Someday girl I don't know when
we're gonna get to that place
Where we really wanna go
and we'll walk in the sun
But till then tramps like us
baby we were born to run"

Music and lyrics by Bruce Springsteen
Recorded and sung by Bruce Springsteen (with the E Street Band)

Bruce Springsteen rented a two-bedroom cottage in Long Branch, New Jersey in 1974 and 1975. It was here he wrote the songs for the album *Born to Run*. Springsteen was just 24 years old at the time. His two previous albums were not much of a commercial success and many thought this could be a do or die album. After 14 months of working on it, his third album was finally released on August 25, 1975 through Columbia Records. The title song itself took 6 months to complete.

With much publicity, *Born to Run,* vaulted into the top 10 in its second week on the charts and soon went Gold. During the week of October 27, 1975, *Time* and *Newsweek* magazines put Springsteen on their covers in the same week. Springsteen has referred to the maturation in his lyrics calling *Born to Run,* "the album where I left behind my adolescent definitions of love and freedom - it was the dividing line." Mark Richardson, writing for Pitchfork in November 2005 on the *Born to Run: 30th Anniversary Edition*, wrote that "*Born to Run* lies entirely on the dreamy and reckless side of maturity and is all the better for it. Every young person should be so lucky to have a time in his or her life when the inflated romanticism of *Born to Run* makes perfect sense." I couldn't agree more with his viewpoint and insight.

For the previous edition of this book I began with The Who and *My Generation. My Generation* was released as a single in November, 1965 at the tail end of the birth of the baby boom generation in America. It was from the groups' debut album, *The Who Sings My Generation*. Roger Daltrey, Pete Townshend, John Entwistle and Keith Moon were 21, 20, 21 and 19 years of age, respectively, when the song hit the airwaves. According to the website Songfacts, Townshend wrote this for rebellious British youths known as "Mods." It expressed their feeling that older people just don't get it. In a 1987 Rolling Stone magazine interview, Townshend explained: "*My Generation* was very much about trying to find a place in society. I was very, very lost. The band was young then. It was believed that its career would be incredibly brief."

2014 is a special year for The Boss as well as that "little ol' band from Texas", the "Piano Man" and maybe you. Let me be the first to wish all a Happy Birthday! I hope this year finds you in good spirits and wonderful health. In addition, 2014 may be the year in which you will turn 65. If so, you've also reached another great milestone in your life. You're now most likely eligible to participate in the U.S. Government's health care insurance program. Congratulations and welcome to Medicare!

The *2010 Patient Protection and Affordable Care Act* and the *Health Care and Education Reconciliation Act of 2010* comprise the principal health care reform legislation known as the *Affordable Care Act* (ACA) or Obamacare. In June 2012, the Supreme Court ruled favorable in a 5-4 narrow vote as constitutional the mandate that all U.S. citizens be required to buy health insurance beginning in 2014. In the ruling for not complying, the penalty was labeled a tax and not a fee. The Court also ruled states would have the option to expand their Medicaid programs, not be mandated as originally written in the ACA legislation.

Health care is a topic in the forefront of media coverage as 2014 unfolds. The initial opening of the Health Insurance Marketplace for individuals was a disaster. The Marketplace for small businesses has now begun with "paper applications" only. As a Medicare beneficiary, <u>NONE</u> of what is happening with these new health exchanges or marketplaces affects Medicare benefits. You don't need to sign up for the new Health Insurance Marketplace if you're already covered by original Medicare, Medicare Advantage, or a Medicare Supplement/Medigap plan.

If you are turning 65 you have probably already become the beneficiary of many unsolicited mailings about the Medicare health insurance program. There is a lot of confusion by many individuals as to exactly how much Medicare costs and what is covered. Some believe it's all free and covers everything. I wish it were that simple. However, Medicare doesn't cover everything and there are costs to you. Costs which can be very significant should you have a major medical event during the year.

Medicare.gov lists over 100 publications, which the federal government produces to describe various aspects of the Medicare program and private health insurance programs which offer additional plans for health coverage which isn't covered by Medicare. Some of these publications are quite lengthy. To be honest with the reader, all these publications are available free online, can be downloaded and printed or can be ordered via telephone.

What this book does provide is a consolidation all that pertinent information you need into one concise unbiased format; allowing you to gain a solid understanding of Medicare, then apply this knowledge to make an intelligent decision about which combination of plans will offer the best coverage and benefits for you.

We are all individuals with a variety of health concerns and income levels. As you read this material think about this simple concept. What is my best case scenario and what is my worst case scenario in terms of costs? In other words, **what could be my total out-of-pocket expenses should I have a major medical event during the year and can I afford that?** Thinking in these terms will keep the total costs you could incur and be responsible for in proper perspective relatively to your income levels and savings which you have.

The discussion of the government's original Medicare program will be specific in its coverage. Discussions of Medicare Advantage, Medicare Supplement/Medigap and Medicare Part D Prescription Drug plans, which are offered by a variety of health care insurance providers, will be kept at a general level. The reason for this is many times premiums, coverage and benefits will vary considerably from state to state and even county to county within the state. This is because the insurance companies are free to charge what competitive force will allow. Medicare Advantage and Medicare Part D drug plans are regulated by the federal government while each state's department of health and insurance services or similar state agency regulates Medicare Supplement/Medigap plans. What options might be offered by plan sponsors in Florida (where I live) may look very different and be priced differently to what is offered in New York, Colorado, Texas, California or Wisconsin for example.

Individuals are going to see significant changes in health care administration over the next five years as Obamacare is fully phased in. Those on Medicare and Medicaid may see changes that few people realize are coming down the road. Beginning in 2013, some physicians began reconsidering their participation in Medicare. Some have notified their patients they are withdrawing from the Medicare program while others have stopped taking new Medicare patients.

Medicare is the elephant in the room. The challenges facing it are really composed of two issues:

(1) the number of projected workers to enrollees is expected to drop from 3.7 in 2010 to 2.4 by 2030 and (2) the skyrocketing cost of health care in general. If steps aren't taken to control both the escalating costs of funding government entitlement programs as well as skyrocketing health care premiums worker's pay, this country may face a devastating health care crisis before it begins the third decade of this century! Bipartisan bickering needs to stop and our congressional leaders need to learn the fine art of compromising again while working together to come up with visionary long term solutions. There is clear and present danger ahead.

Advances in biomedical science, an integrated process of employing the principles of biology, biochemistry, physiology and other basic sciences to solve problems in clinical medicine have significantly helped in extending our life spans. Through biomedical engineering, advances in the design and functionality of artificial limbs have greatly improved quality of life issues for those in need of limb replacement. This is now beginning to extend to organ replacement. These advances are amazing compared to what existed just ten years ago.

However, life extension is not without its costs. Many of the maladies people face today would not have been survivable twenty years ago. These advances in medical technology are rapidly driving up health care costs. Just think of the types of medical care and procedures which may be available twenty years from now. Will insurance cover them and, if so, at what cost? Americans will likely continue to have the capacity to live longer than their forbearers. That's the good news. The bad news is many will likely live their lives with some sort of chronic illness such as obesity, some form of cardiovascular disease or neurological degenerative process, skeletal issues requiring orthopedic procedures or Type-2 diabetes, which will require ongoing medical care.

Each year Fidelity Benefits Consulting, a division of Fidelity Investments, calculates its annual retiree health care costs estimate. For 2013, it's estimated a 65 year couple retiring this year will spend $220,000 in out-of-pocket medical expenses while in retirement. This is down 8% from the 2012 estimate of $240,000. This decrease in estimated health care costs was in part due to lower-than-expected Medicare spending in recent years, as well as a reduction in projected Medicare spending in the near future.

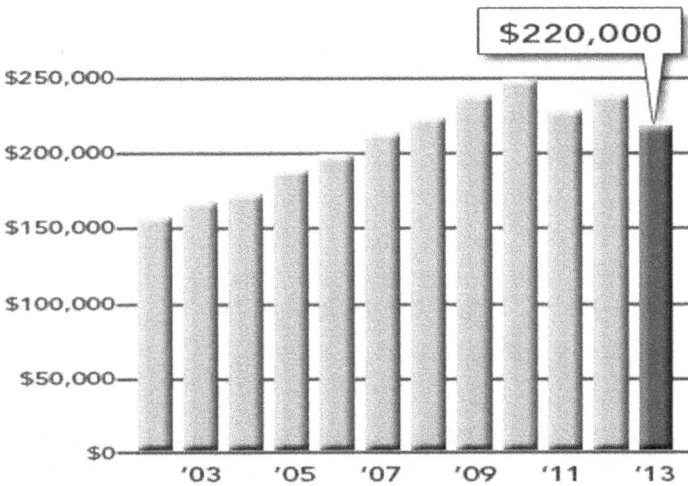

Source: Fidelity Benefits Consulting, 2013

Their analysis is based on a hypothetical couple retiring at age 65 with average life expectancies of 82 and 85 female for the male and female, respectively. Estimates are calculated for "average" retirees but may be more or less depending on actual health status, area of residence, and longevity. It assumes individuals do not have employer-provided retiree health care coverage but qualify for Medicare. The calculation takes into account cost sharing provisions (such as deductibles and coinsurance) associated with Medicare Part A and Part B (inpatient and outpatient medical insurance). It also considers Medicare Part D (prescription drug coverage) premiums and out-of-pocket costs, as well as certain services excluded by Medicare. **This estimate does not include other health-related expenses such as over-the-counter medications, most dental services and long-term care, which are NOT covered by Medicare.**

Fidelity's health care cost estimate had decreased only once before. That was in 2011, when the estimate declined $20,000 due to a one-time adjustment driven by Medicare changes that reduced out-of-pocket expenses for prescription drugs for many seniors. Between 2002 and 2012, the estimate had increased an average of 6% annually. In 2001, Fidelity's estimate was $160,000. Making the wrong choices could have serious consequences as you age and your health changes; stressing family finances to the limit and altering your retirement lifestyle.

Most would agree baby boomers, an estimated **78,000,000** who were born from 1946 through 1965, will have a profound effect on health care in this country in the years to come. The first boomers were eligible to begin receiving early Social Security benefits in 2008. In 2011, those same boomers became the first wave eligible to qualify for Medicare. It's estimated that beginning with 2011, 10,000 baby boomers will turn 65 each day and every day for the next 18 years. By 2030, 80 million people may be enrolled in the Medicare program, up from 47 million in 2010. This is a near doubling in just 20 years!

Health care costs have the potential to torpedo many future retirement plans if individuals don't do some thoughtful planning ahead of time to ensure they are both adequately protected against rising health risks and have the ability to continuing making premium payments to ensure continued coverage and benefits. If not, they may face a radically different lifestyle during their later retirement years than they expected. The saying is true. If you don't have your health, all the money you have doesn't mean that much. Living becomes an agonizing ordeal each day.

This book is one part in a trilogy I have written covering the subjects of Medicare, health insurance and Social Security. While the focus of this book is on one aspect of the holistic health care process, Medicare; the second book in the series covers general health insurance choices, including the new Health Insurance Marketplace. The third book in the series will explore Social Security claiming strategies. Two other books covering investing and financial planning, tentatively titled; *The Alchemy of Market Cycles: Footprints in Time or Stepping-stones to the Future* and *Avoiding Premature Financial Depletion through Longevity Planning,* respectively, will be published later in 2014.

Since we started the section with a reference to "The Boss" and his music, let's end with taking a look at some phenomenal artists who were born in 1949 and who turn that momentous age of 65 throughout 2014. Happy Birthday to all and thanks for the great, wonderful and magical music that's still played today!

- Steve Perry (Journey)
- Ross Valory (Journey)
- Chick Churchill (Ten Years After)
- Eddie Hardin (Spencer Davis Group)
- Jerry Harrison (Talking Heads)
- Mike Gibbons (Badfinger)
- Eddie Money
- Fran Sheehan (Boston)
- Ric Ocasek (Cars)
- Milan Williams (Commodores)
- John Oats (Hall & Oats)
- Billy Joel
- Overend Watts (Mott the Hoople)
- William Sputnik Spooner (Grateful Dead)
- Dusty Hill (ZZ Top)
- John Illsley (Dire Straits)
- Jack Ryland (Three Dog Night)
- Frank Beard (ZZ Top)
- Alan White (Yes)
- Michael Lutz (Brownville Station)
- Lionel Richie (Commodores)
- Alan Osmond (Osmond Brothers)
- Larry Junstrom (.38 Special)
- Dave Smally (Raspberries)
- Wally Bryson (Raspberries)
- Mike Vale (Tommy James & The Shondells)
- Terry "Geezer" Butler (Black Sabbath)
- Roger Taylor (Queen)
- Steve Peregrine Took (T-Rex)

- Simon Kirke (Bad Company)
- Eric Carmen (Raspberries)
- Sib Hashian (Boston)
- Gene Simmons (KISS)
- David "Clem" Clempson (Humble Pie)
- Barriemore Barlow (Jethro Tull)
- Steve Gaines (Lynyrd Skynyrd) d. 1977
- Kerry Livgren (Kansas)
- David Coverdale (Deep Purple & Whitesnake)
- **Bruce Springsteen**
- Lindsey Buckingham (Fleetwood Mac)
- Greg Douglas (Steve Miller Band)
- Craig McGregor (Foghat)
- Gary Richrath (REO Speedwagon)
- Mickey Thomas (Jefferson Airplane & Starship)
- Cliff Williams (AC/DC)
- Billy Gibbons (ZZ Top)
- Paul Rogers (Free & Bad Company)
- Maurice Gibb (Bee Gees) d.2003
- Robin Gibb (Bee Gees) d. 2012

Source: musicorb.com for listed birthdays

Cheers! Here's to <u>your</u> healthy and full-filled retirement or whatever you wish to call it.

Stephen

Stephen J. Stellhorn
December 2013
Tampa, Florida

"If you look at the studies coming out of the Congressional Budget Office, the number one thing that's going to blow a hole in the federal deficit as we go forward 20, 30 years is government spending on healthcare."

Christina Romer
Professor of Economics – University of California at Berkeley
Former Chairperson – Council of Economic Advisors
President Barack Obama Administration

CHAPTER ONE

THE COST OF HEALTH CARE

According to the Centers for Medicare and Medicaid Services (CMS), in their National Health Expenditures Projections 2011-2021 report, total health care spending in the U.S. is expected to reach $4.8 trillion in 2021. This is up from $2.6 trillion in 2010 and $75 billion in 1970. From the Bureau of Labor Statistics medical costs have risen, on average, 5.7% per year for the past twenty years. This is double the rate of inflation as measured by the CPI.

How does health care spending and life expectancy rates in the United States compare with those of other developed countries? The facts are not what you might expect. In 2009, health care spending per person was far higher in the U.S. than any other industrialized country, at nearly $8,000 per person. This probably isn't a surprise to most of you. Switzerland was second at roughly $5,000 per person while New Zealand was the lowest at just under $3,000 per person. Figure 1.1 below illustrates a number of industrialized countries and their health care expense per person along with their estimated life expectancy rates for 2009.

Figure 1.1 Health Care Spending Per Person and Life Expectancy

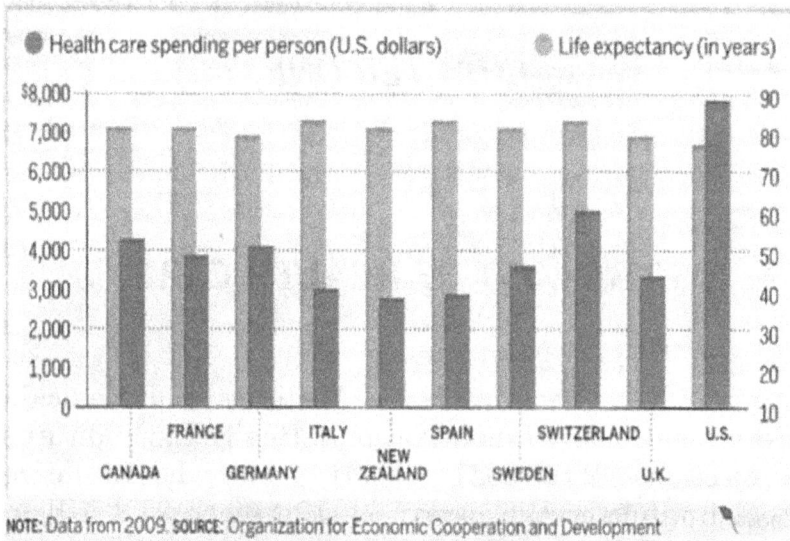

Courtesy: *MONEY magazine, October 2011*
Source: *OECD*

What you might not expect, from the chart above, is Americans aren't necessarily healthier as evidenced by our life expectancy rate which is the lowest.

As measured by GDP, the overall costs for health care have been expanding at a rate of two percentage points faster than the overall economy. This problem will only get worse in the coming decade as aging baby boomers flood the Medicare system and longer life spans add more years of medical care. Americans, age

65 in 2012 have an average life expectancy of 18 additional years.

Under the current law most Americans collect far more from the Medicare system than they pay in. According to calculations by the Urban Institute, a married couple who retired in 2011 can expect to receive $350,000 in lifetime benefits. To receive this benefit they only paid in about $150,000 in Medicare taxes. A couple who were 46 in 2011 can expect to receive $525,000 in benefits when they retire at 65. Their cost in Medicare taxes; just over $200,000. This example assumes a two-earner couple; one with $69,600 income and the other with $43,500 in income during 2011.

In 1880 there were only 1.7 million individuals 65 and older. Even by 1940, 60 years later, there were still less than 10 million individuals 65 and older.

Figure 1.2 U.S. Population By Age 65+ - 1900-2050

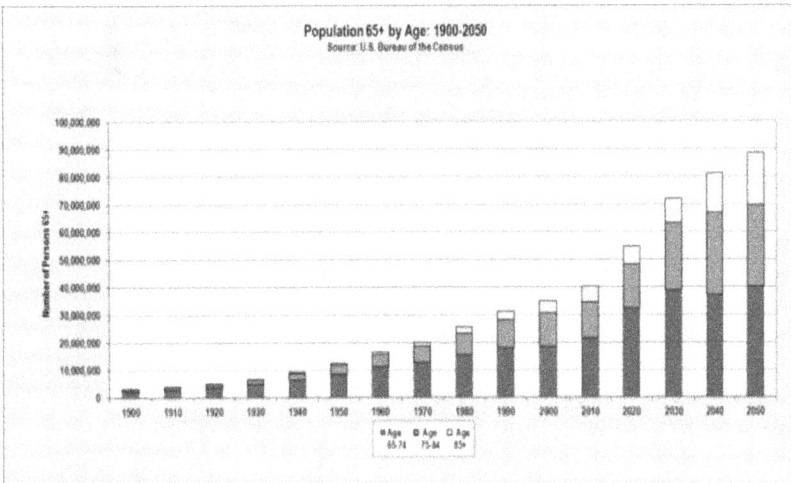

Courtesy of U.S. Administration on Aging
Source: U.S. Census Bureau

However, by 1970, just 30 years later, the figure had double and by 2010 the figure had doubled again to just over 40 million. Between 2000 and 2010, the population, age 65 and over, increased at a faster rate (15.1%) than the total U.S. population (9.7%). According to the U.S. Administration on Aging, by 2050 there will be an estimated 88.5 million individuals 65 and older, as illustrated in Figure 1.2 on the previous page.

In Figure 1.3 below, the future percentage makeup of GDP is illustrated. The large area at the bottom of the graph, labeled "everything else" includes Social Security.

Figure 1.3 Estimation of Future Percentage
Makeup of GDP: 2011-2051

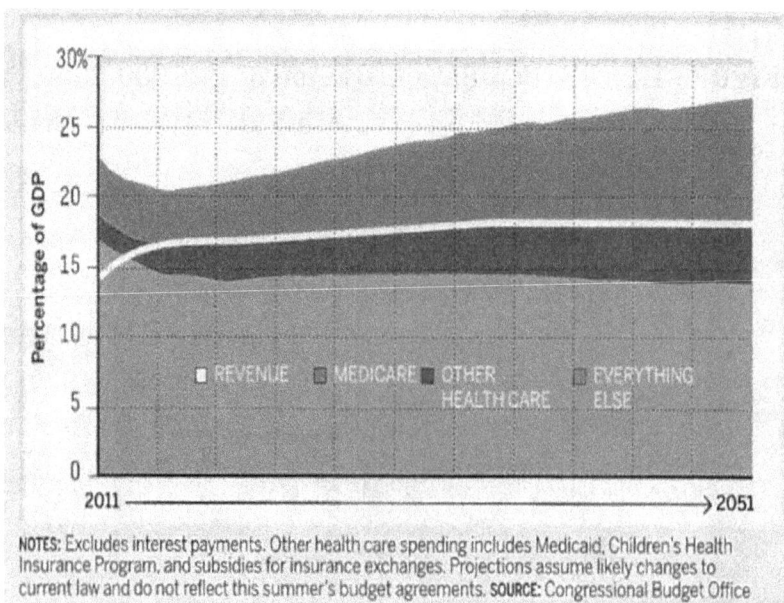

NOTES: Excludes interest payments. Other health care spending includes Medicaid, Children's Health Insurance Program, and subsidies for insurance exchanges. Projections assume likely changes to current law and do not reflect this summer's budget agreements. SOURCE: Congressional Budget Office

Courtesy: MONEY magazine, October 2011
Source: CBO

While Social Security is an important issue, it pales in comparison to the rising costs for entitlements like Medicare. By 2030, maintaining benefits at current levels would push government spending to 24% of the economy; with even higher percentages as the years go on. Taxes on the other hand are expected to generate revenues equal to only 18% of the economy. Clearly this is an unsustainable glide path in the long run.

While there is a great deal of dissension in Washington on a variety of issues other than health care, both parties agree that controlling Medicare costs is critical to controlling the growing budget gap and future fiscal deficits. Even with reforms, fixing Medicare will be tough. In the end there will need to be some combination of premium/tax increases, increases in copays and coinsurance, higher deductibles, cap limit increases and possible changes in the eligibility age to receive these benefits. The bottom line; expect and plan for higher costs and less benefits! The issues are serious and the challenge for Congress and the President is determining the right combination of choices.

When employer-sponsored health insurance plans are examined, the trends are not good. Since 1999, inflation and workers' earnings have risen by cumulative percentages of 40% and 50%, respectively. During the same period, cumulative percentage increases for health insurance premiums and worker' contributions to premiums have seen a three-fold increase since 1999. In Figure 1.4, on the next page, the graph plots the *cumulative* increases in health insurance premiums, workers' contributions to premiums, inflation and workers' earnings over a fourteen year period.

5

Figure 1.4 Cumulative Increases in Health
Insurance Premiums, Workers'
Contributions to Premiums, Inflation
and Workers' Earnings 1999-2013

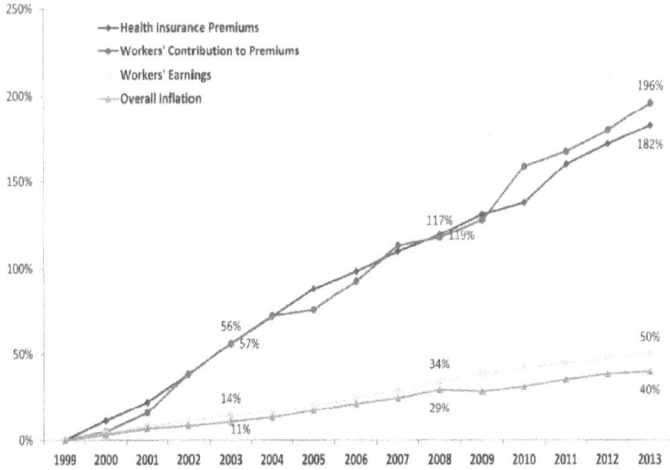

SOURCE: Kaiser/HRET Survey of Employer-Sponsored Health Benefits, 1999-2013. Bureau of Labor Statistics, Consumer Price Index, U.S. City Average of Annual Inflation (April to April), 1999-2013; Bureau of Labor Statistics, Seasonally Adjusted Data from the Current Employment Statistics Survey, 1999-2013 (April to April).

Courtesy: The Kaiser Foundation; 2013 Employer Health Benefit Survey

When we examine average annual health care premiums for single and family coverage over the same time horizon we see an equally disturbing picture in cost trends. These are the total of both the employee and employer contribution.

As illustrated in Figure 1.5, in the graph on the next page, in 1999 the average premium for single and family health insurance coverage was $2,196 and $5,791, respectively. Fourteen years later in 2013, these average annual premiums for single and family coverage had risen to $5,884 and $16,351 per year, respectively.

Figure 1.5 Average Annual Health Insurance Premiums for Single and Family Coverage 1999-2013

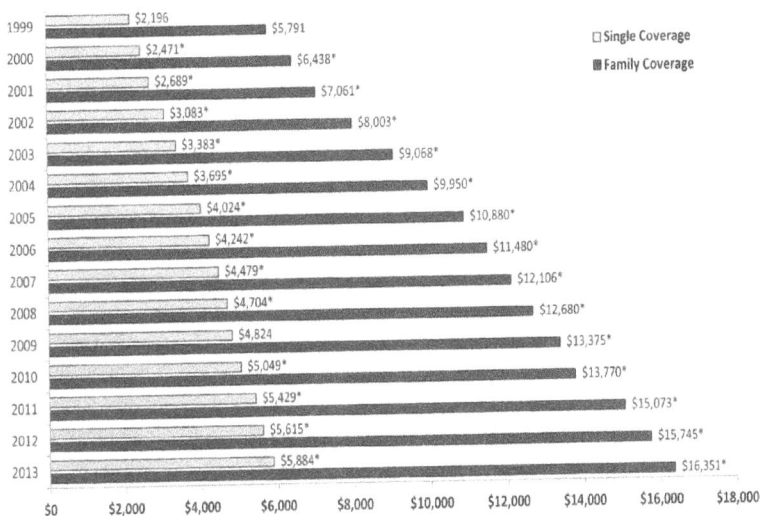

* Estimate is statistically different from estimate for the previous year shown (p<.05).

SOURCE: Kaiser/HRET Survey of Employer-Sponsored Health Benefits, 1999-2013.

Courtesy: The Kaiser Foundation; 2013 Employer Health Benefit Survey

The *International Federation of Health Plans (iFHP)* was founded in 1968 by a group of health insurance industry leaders and is now the leading global network for the industry. The federation is based in London, England. Through its diverse membership of over one hundred health insurers, in twenty-five countries, the iFHP is in a unique position to observe cost trends in health care products and services. They recently released their *2012 Comparative Price Report*, which is their fourth annual survey. This report contains 28 graphs which display the prices for the cost of specific hospital costs, medical procedures, physician fees and prescription drugs, compiled from data collected by iFHP member plans. The U.S. numbers are based on an aggregate of over 100 million paid claims across multiple payers. What follows is a sampling of eleven graphs reproduced from that report, which can be obtained from the iFHP website at www.ifhp.com.

Figure 1.6 Cost Per Hospital <u>Day</u>

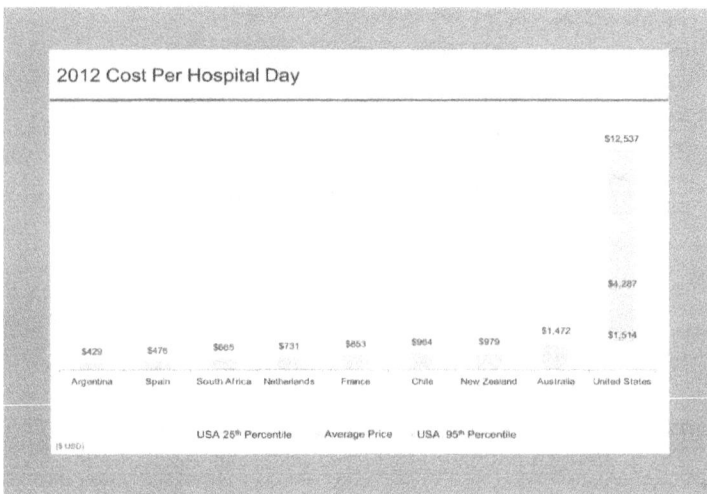

Courtesy: The International Federation of Health Plans; 2012 Comparative Price Report

Figure 1.7 Angiogram Imaging Cost

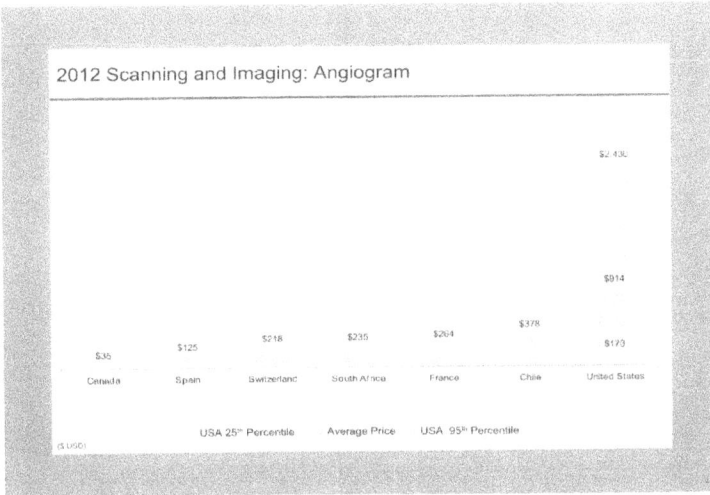

2012 Scanning and Imaging: Angiogram

						$2,430
						$914
					$378	
		$218	$235	$264		$173
	$125					
$35						
Canada	Spain	Switzerland	South Africa	France	Chile	United States

USA 25ᵗʰ Percentile   Average Price   USA 95ᵗʰ Percentile

($ USD)

*Courtesy: The International Federation of Health Plans;
2012 Comparative Price Report*

Figure 1.8 Routine Office Visit Cost

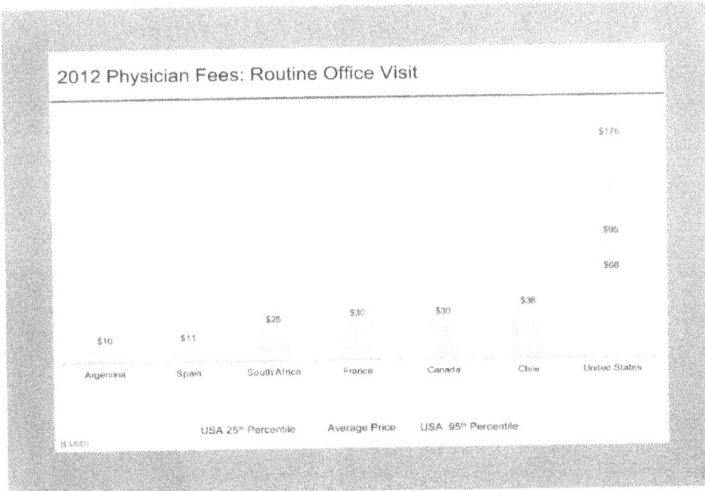

2012 Physician Fees: Routine Office Visit

						$176
						$95
						$68
					$36	
		$25	$30	$30		
$10	$11					
Argentina	Spain	South Africa	France	Canada	Chile	United States

USA 25ᵗʰ Percentile   Average Price   USA 95ᵗʰ Percentile

($ USD)

*Courtesy: The International Federation of Health Plans;
2012 Comparative Price Report*

Figure 1.9 Coronary Artery Bypass Surgery Cost

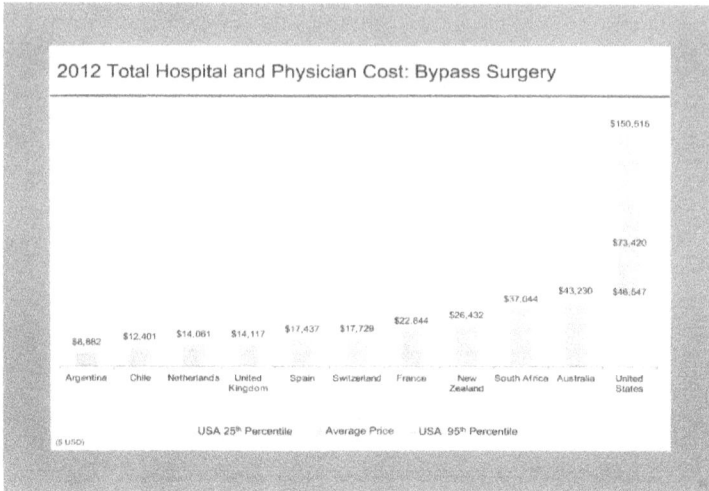

2012 Total Hospital and Physician Cost: Bypass Surgery

$150,515

$73,420

$46,547
$43,230
$37,044
$26,432
$22,844
$17,729
$17,437
$14,117
$14,061
$12,401
$8,882

Argentina, Chile, Netherlands, United Kingdom, Spain, Switzerland, France, New Zealand, South Africa, Australia, United States

USA 25th Percentile   Average Price   USA 95th Percentile

($ USD)

Courtesy: The International Federation of Health Plans;
2012 Comparative Price Report

Figure 1.10 MRI Imaging Cost

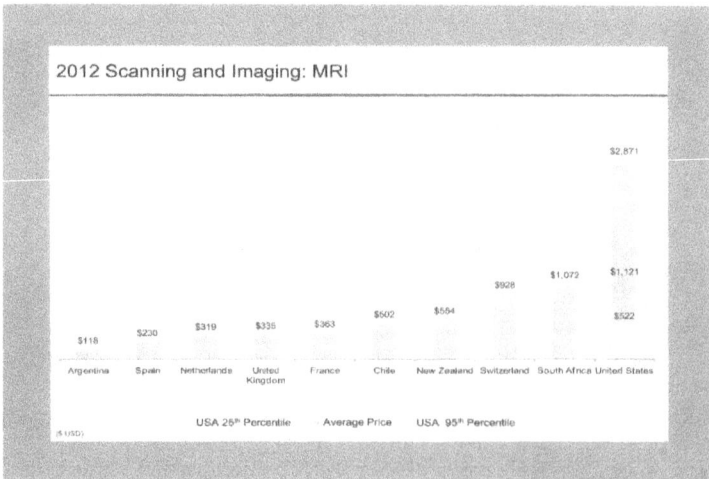

2012 Scanning and Imaging: MRI

$2,871

$1,121
$1,072
$928
$584
$522
$502
$363
$338
$319
$230
$118

Argentina, Spain, Netherlands, United Kingdom, France, Chile, New Zealand, Switzerland, South Africa, United States

USA 25th Percentile   Average Price   USA 95th Percentile

($ USD)

Courtesy: The International Federation of Health Plans
2012 Comparative Price Report

Figure 1.11 Hip Replacement Cost

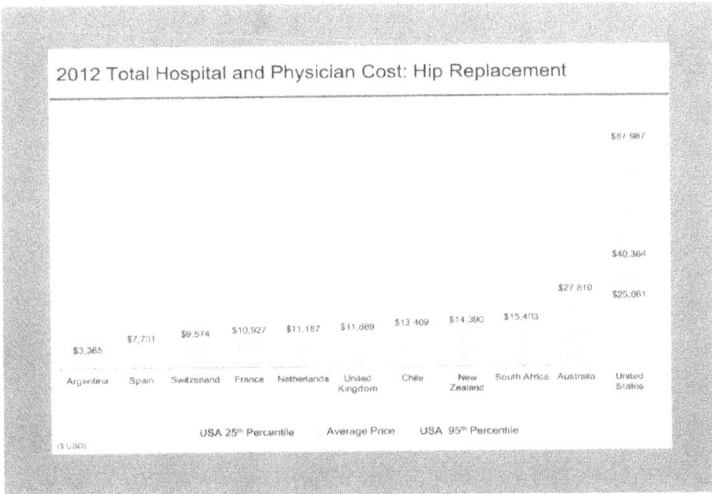

2012 Total Hospital and Physician Cost: Hip Replacement

$87,987

$40,364

$27,810

$25,061

$3,365 $7,731 $9,574 $10,927 $11,187 $11,889 $13,409 $14,390 $15,470

Argentina   Spain   Switzerland   France   Netherlands   United Kingdom   Chile   New Zealand   South Africa   Australia   United States

USA 25th Percentile   Average Price   USA 95th Percentile

($ USD)

Courtesy: The International Federation of Health Plans;
2012 Comparative Price Report

Figure 1.12 Cataract Surgery Cost

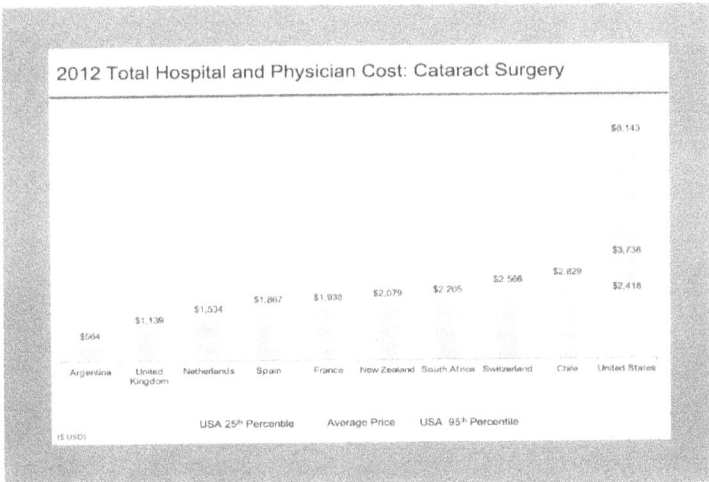

2012 Total Hospital and Physician Cost: Cataract Surgery

$8,145

$3,738

$2,829

$2,586 $2,418

$2,205

$2,079

$1,938

$1,867

$1,534

$1,139

$564

Argentina   United Kingdom   Netherlands   Spain   France   New Zealand   South Africa   Switzerland   Chile   United States

USA 25th Percentile   Average Price   USA 95th Percentile

($ USD)

Courtesy: The International Federation of Health Plans;
2012 Comparative Price Report

Figure 1.13 Colonoscopy Cost

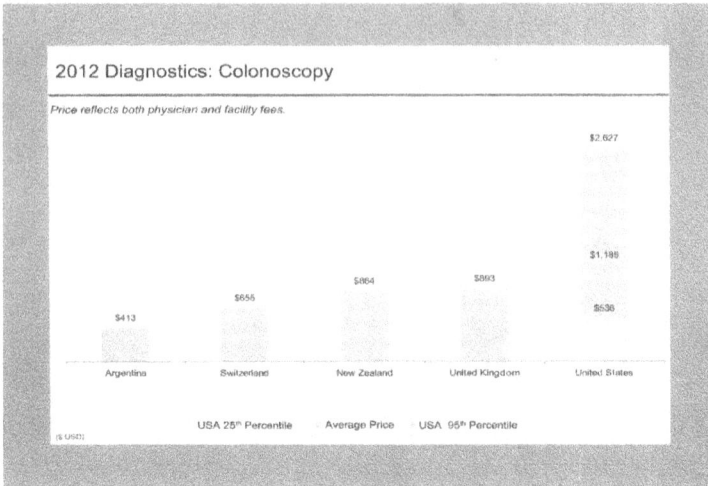

2012 Diagnostics: Colonoscopy

Price reflects both physician and facility fees.

$2,627

$1,199

$864 $893

$655

$536

$413

Argentina Switzerland New Zealand United Kingdom United States

USA 25ᵗʰ Percentile   Average Price   USA 95ᵗʰ Percentile

($ USD)

Courtesy: The International Federation of Health Plans;
2012 Comparative Price Report

Figure 1.14 Cymbalta Drug Cost

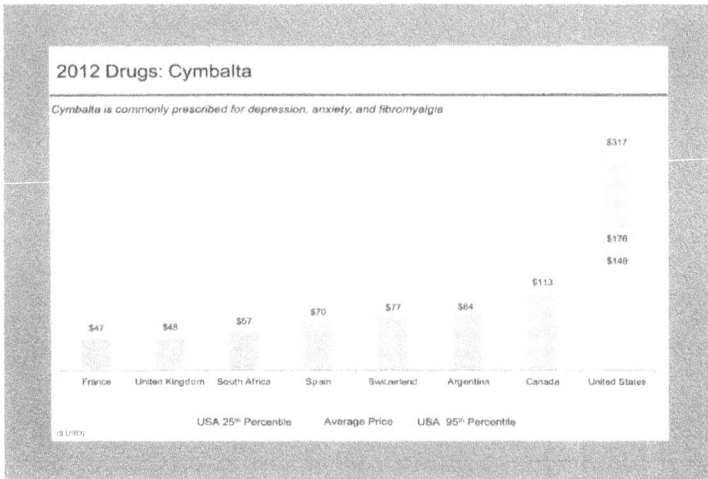

2012 Drugs: Cymbalta

Cymbalta is commonly prescribed for depression, anxiety, and fibromyalgia

$317

$176

$149

$113

$70 $77 $84

$57

$47 $48

France United Kingdom South Africa Spain Switzerland Argentina Canada United States

USA 25ᵗʰ Percentile   Average Price   USA 95ᵗʰ Percentile

($ USD)

Courtesy: The International Federation of Health Plans;
2012 Comparative Price Report

Figure 1.15 Nexium Drug Cost

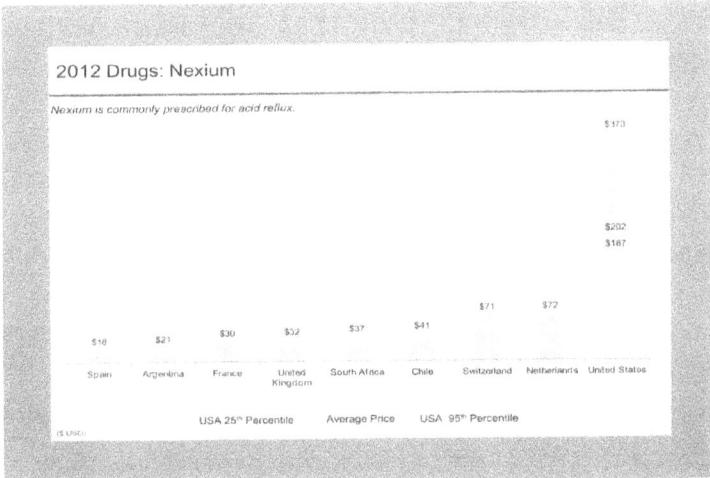

Courtesy: The International Federation of Health Plans;
2012 Comparative Price Report

Figure 1.16 Lipitor Drug Cost

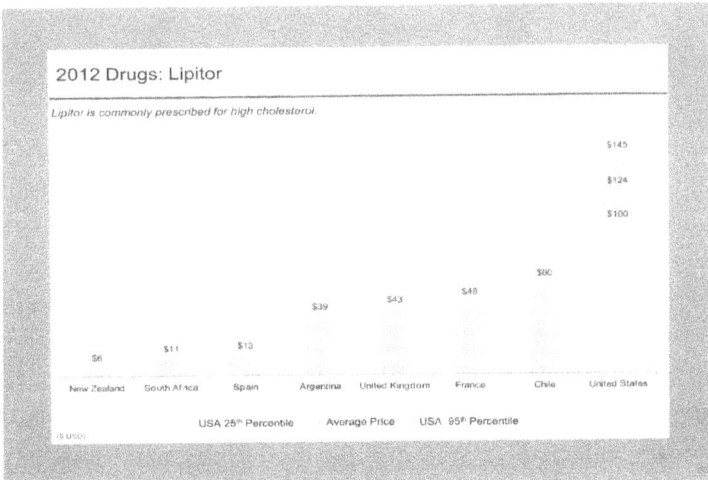

Courtesy: The International Federation of Health Plans;
2012 Comparative Price Report

As you can see from the previous graphs, the cost to obtain various medical and health care needs in the U.S. is far greater than that in other developed countries. While these graphs look at purely the costs of various aspects of health care, they imply nothing regarding the quality and delivery of that health care.

Recently, at the 2014 World Economic Forum in Davos, Switzerland, the CEO of Aetna, Mark Bertolini characterization that "medical expenses remain out of control in the U.S., where Americans have an unsustainable attitude that ignores the increasing cost of health care." The health care system needs to shift to a system which pays for the quality of care rather than the quantity.

According to the January 2014 issue of Health Affairs, for the fourth consecutive year, growth in health care spending remained low, increasing by 3.7% in 2012 to $2.8 trillion. At the same time, the share of the economy devoted to health care fell slightly to 17.2% from 17.3%.

HEALTH CARE DEMAND CURVES

The Bureau of Labor Statistics (BLS) produces the Consumer Expenditure Survey (CE) program which consists of two surveys, the Quarterly Interview Survey and the Diary Survey. These surveys provide information on the buying habits of American consumers, including data on their expenditures, income, and consumer unit (families and single consumers) characteristics. The survey asks 5,000 respondents to list all income and expenditures out of their personal budgets for a period of 6 weeks. From sodas, movies and mortgage payments to car, pizza,

14

and insurance expenses - literally anything paid out of the household is recorded. Respondents are then asked demographic questions such age, education, number of children, and where they live. From this data we can see how people spend money at different ages and on what products and services.

Harry S. Dent, Jr. has done some of the best research and analysis I've seen regarding long-term consumer buying habits and demographic trends. In 1988, Dent developed a new long term indicator to predict economic activity based on spending and birth rate patterns. New generations come along every 40 years. In his research Dent found that as individual's age, they move through predictable earning, spending and productivity cycles.

As you might expect demand for health care is the highest after 50. It begins to creep up from the early 30s to 40s but begins to take a dramatic rise after 50. From the data Dent has collected from the CE survey, he has created demand curves for multiple products and services. These demand curves simply graph the average age of the household on the x-axis and on the y-axis graphs the dollars spent per year on a product or service. Several demand curves for select health care expenditures are presented next. I've organized them according to the age when a person may be in need of the specific product or service. We're not going to explain each one because they are pretty self-explanatory. What's important to think about is the age where peak demand occurs and when it finally begins to trend lower. The nine graphs on the following pages are courtesy of H.S. Dent. If you're interested in more demand curves you can view the PDF file at Dent's website at www.hsdent.com.

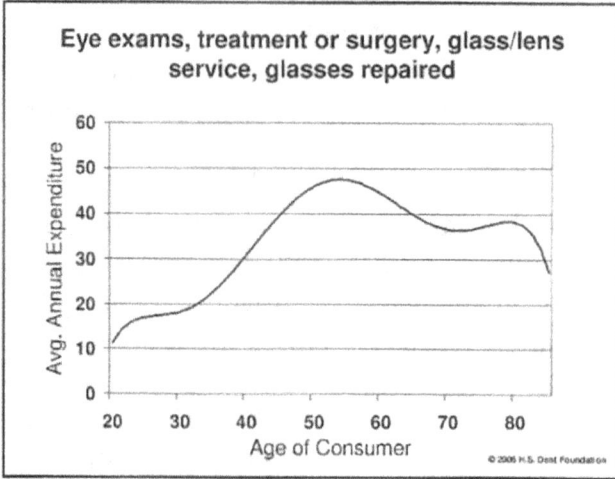

Eye exams, treatment or surgery, glass/lens service, glasses repaired

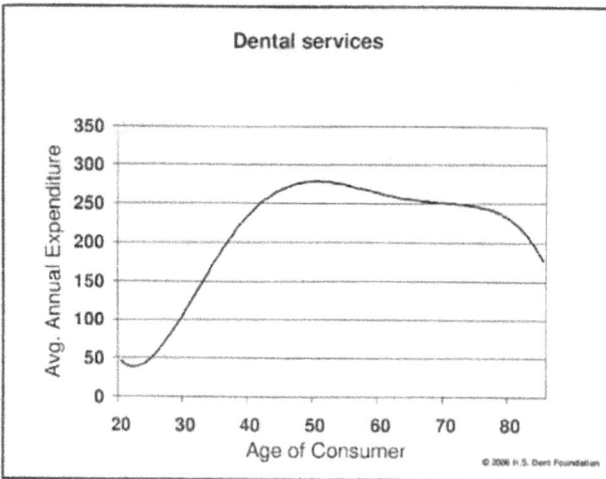

Dental services

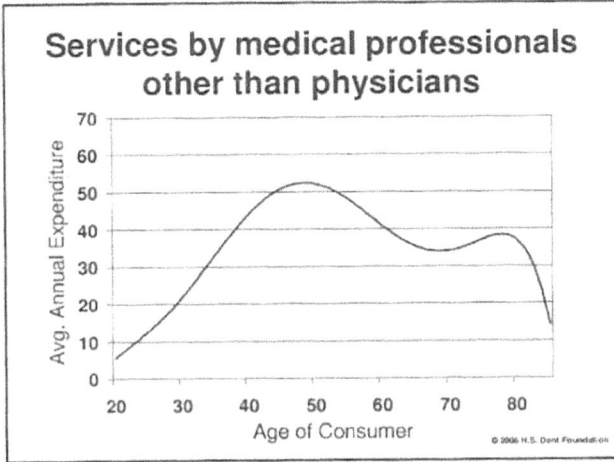

Services by medical professionals other than physicians

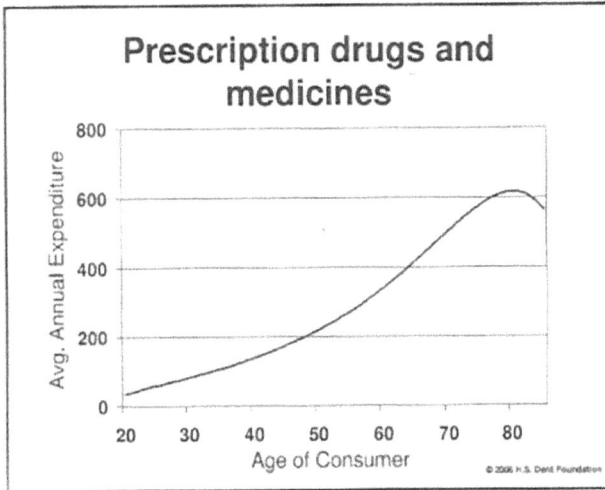

Prescription drugs and medicines

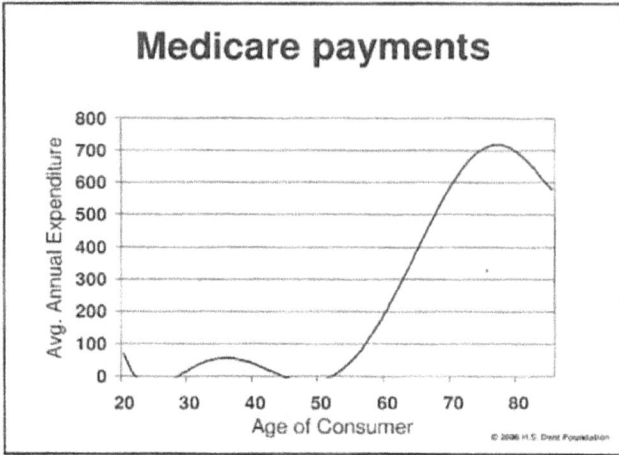

Medicare payments

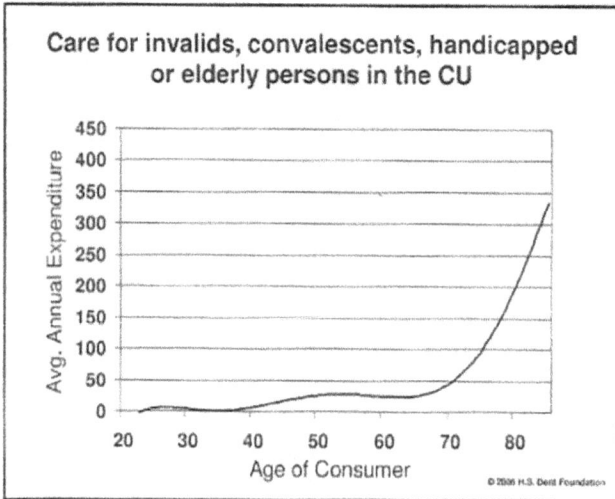

Care for invalids, convalescents, handicapped or elderly persons in the CU

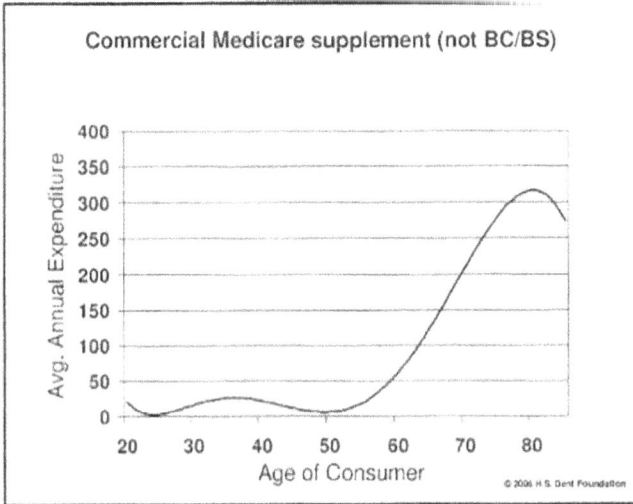

Commercial Medicare supplement (not BC/BS)

© 2006 H.S. Dent Foundation

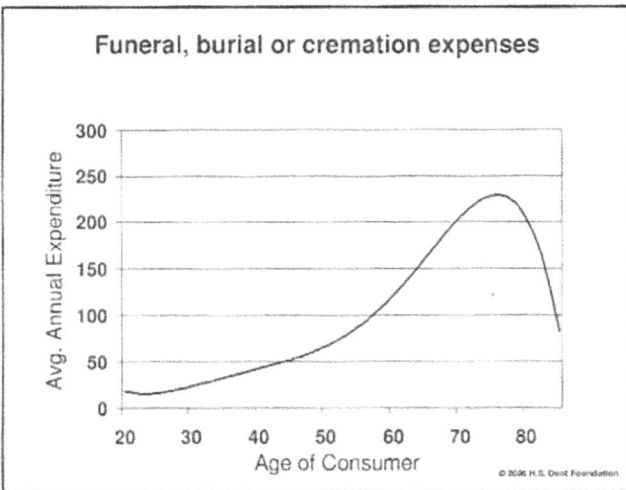

Funeral, burial or cremation expenses

© 2006 H.S. Dent Foundation

19

"It worries me about our unwillingness to really address reforms and modernization in Medicare. This thing was designed 37 years ago. It has not evolved to keep pace with current medical technology."

John Sununu
Chair of Republican Party of New Hampshire
White House Chief of Staff - President George H.W. Bush Administration
75th Governor of New Hampshire

CHAPTER TWO

THE MEDICARE PROGRAM

Congress created Medicare under Title XVIII, Health Insurance for the Aged and Disabled as part of the Social Security Act and Medicaid under Title XIX in 1965 to provide health insurance to people age 65 and older or who are disabled regardless of income or medical history. The bill was signed into law by President Lyndon Johnson during the summer of 1965. In 1972, Congress expanded Medicare eligibility to younger people who have permanent disabilities and receive Social Security Disability Insurance (SSDI) payments and those who have end-stage renal disease (ESRD). Congress further expanded Medicare eligibility in 2001 to cover younger people with amyotrophic lateral sclerosis (ALS, or Lou Gehrig's disease). Beginning in 2007, as required in the *Medicare Prescription Drug, Improvement and Modernization Act of 2003*, the Part B premium a beneficiary pays each month to cover medically-necessary services would be means-tested and based on annual income.

The Centers for Medicare and Medicaid Services (CMS), a federal agency within the U.S. Department of Health and Human Services (HHS) of the federal government, administers Medicare, Medicaid, the State Children's Health Insurance Program (SCHIP), the Clinical Laboratory Improvement Amendments (CLIA) and now the Health Insurance Marketplaces. CMS creates and monitors detailed rules regarding how the Medicare insurance program should operate so the program meets the best interest of its beneficiaries. Along with the Departments of Labor and Treasury, CMS also implements the insurance reform provisions of the *Health Insurance Portability and Accountability Act of 1996 (HIPAA).*

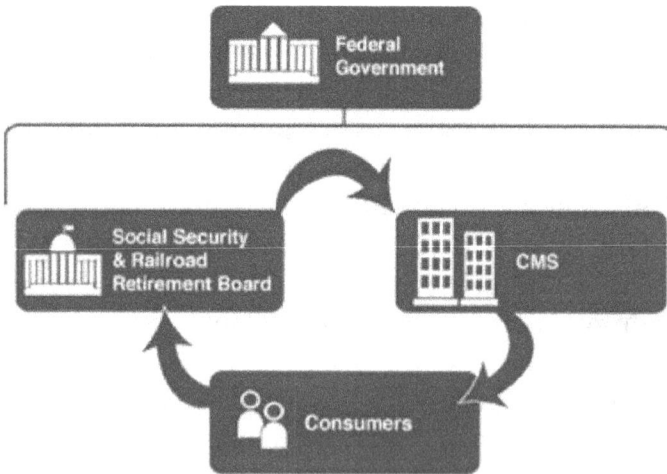

Courtesy: UnitedHealthcare® Medicare Solutions

The Social Security Administration (SSA) and the Railroad Retirement Board (RRB) are responsible for determining Medicare eligibility, enrolling consumers and processing premium payments for the Medicare program.

As illustrated in Figure 2.1 below, in 2010, Medicare provided health insurance to 47 million Americans. People age 65 and older accounted for 39 million of these Americans while 8 million were younger with disabilities.

Figure 2.1 Medicare Enrollment: 1966-2010

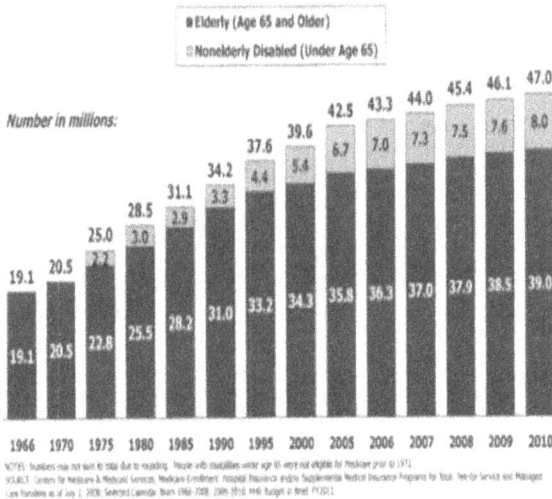

Medicare is a federal health insurance program covering an estimated 47 million people in 2010, including 39 million Americans ages 65 and older and 8 million people with permanent disabilities who are under age 65. With the aging and growth of the U.S. population, the number of Medicare beneficiaries more than doubled between 1966 and 2000 and is projected to double yet again to 80 million by 2030, according to Medicare program actuaries.

Source: Kaiser Family Foundation; Medicare Chartbook Fourth Edition, 2010

In Figure 2.2, on the next page, the percentage of Medicare beneficiaries of each state's population is illustrated. There are five states with between 19%

and 21%. West Virginia and Maine have the highest percentage of Medicare beneficiaries at 21%. Alaska has the lowest percentage of beneficiaries at just 10% followed by Utah at 11%.

Figure 2.2 Medicare Beneficiaries as a Percent of State Populations, 2012

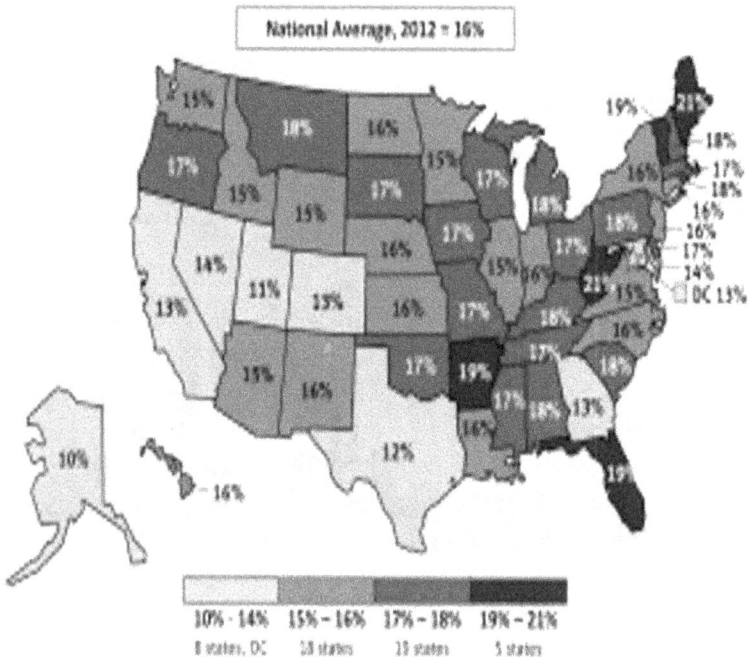

Source: Kaiser Family Foundation

Most Medicare beneficiaries live on modest incomes as is illustrated in Figure 2.3 on the next page. In 2006, 64% of Medicare beneficiaries had incomes less than $30,000. Only 3% had incomes greater than $100,000. Even by 2009, median personal income for persons 65 and older had increased to only $31,354.

Figure 2.3 Median per Capita Income Among
Medicare Beneficiaries, 2013

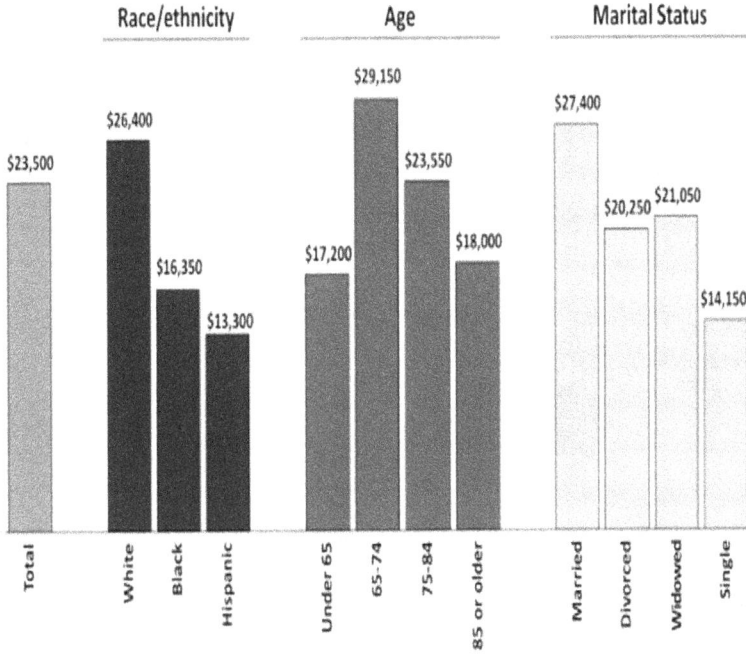

NOTE: Total household income for couples is split equally between husbands and wives to estimate income for married beneficiaries.
SOURCE: Urban Institute / Kaiser Family Foundation analysis, 2013.

*Source: Kaiser Family Foundation; Income and Assets of
Medicare Beneficiaries, 2013 -2030*

According to the Kaiser Family Foundation, 50% of all
Medicare beneficiaries had incomes below $23,500 in
2013. There were 25% with incomes below $14,000. At
the other end of the income spectrum, 5% had incomes
about $93,000 with 1% having incomes above
$171,650.

When Kaiser examined savings of Medicare
beneficiaries, 50% had savings below $61,400 in 2013.
There were 25% who had savings below $11,300 and

8% had $0 in savings or were in debt. At the other end of the spectrum, 5% had savings above $1,112,950 with 1% having more than $3,423,800. This analysis includes retirement account holdings, savings accounts, stocks and bonds. Figure 2.4 below displays the median per capita savings among Medicare beneficiaries.

Figure 2.4 Median per Capita Savings Among Medicare Beneficiaries, 2013

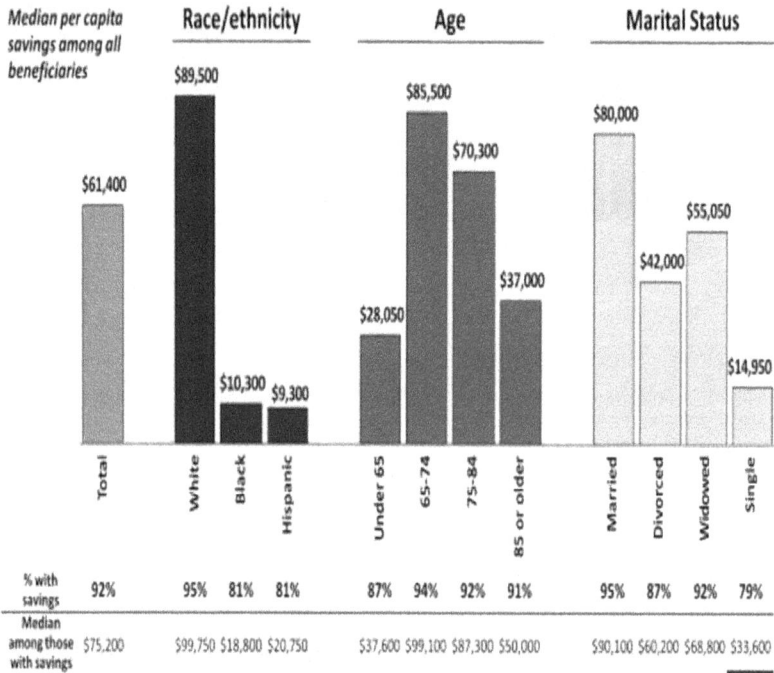

Source: Kaiser Family Foundation; Income and Assets of Medicare Beneficiaries, 2013 -2030

COMPOSITION OF MEDICARE HEALTH COVERAGE

The Medicare health insurance program is composed of six programs. These programs consist of:

- Part A – Hospitalization Insurance
- Part B – Medical Insurance
- Part C – Medicare Advantage Plans
- Part D – Medicare Prescription Drug Plans
- Medicare Cost Plans
- Programs of All-Inclusive Care for the Elderly (PACE)

Medicare Part A and Part B are commonly referred to as original Medicare. Everything else is referred to as Medicare health plans.

The CMS administers original Medicare Part A and Part B and is responsible for approving claims (services and prices) and pays a portion of its approved amounts, subject to certain deductibles, copays and coinsurance.

The Medicare Advantage Part C and Medicare Prescription Drug Part D coverage plans are offered by private health insurance companies, approved by Medicare. There may also be subject to certain deductibles, copays and coinsurance. CMS regulates all aspects of the Medicare Part C and Part D plans, including plan benefits, marketing and enrollment processes. This also extends to insurance companies, insurance agents and in their marketing, sales and educational events presented to consumers.

Medicare cost plans are available in certain areas of the country. PACE is a Medicare and Medicaid program offered in many states which allows individuals who otherwise need a nursing home level of care to remain in the community. To qualify for PACE you need to meet these conditions:

- You're 55 or older.
- You live in the service area of a PACE organization.
- You're certified by your state as needing a nursing home level of care.
- You're able to live safely in the community with the help of PACE services at the time you join.

PACE provides coverage for prescription drugs, physician or other health care provider visits, transportation, home care, hospital visits and even nursing home stays whenever necessary. If you have Medicaid you will not have to pay a monthly premium for the long-term care portion of the PACE benefit. If you have Medicare but not Medicaid, you will be charged a monthly premium to cover the long-term care portion of the PACE benefit.

Medicare Supplement/Medigap plans are not part of the government's Medicare program but are plans offered by private insurance companies which fill in the gaps which original Medicare doesn't cover.

With Medicare, consumers can choose different coverage options to suit their medical needs. We will cover the details for each of these in subsequent chapters along with their specific enrollment periods. As you can see in the pie chart in Figure 2.5, on the next page, as of December 2011 only 8% of individuals were enrolled in only original Medicare Part A and Part B with no additional coverage options.

Figure 2.5 Post Age 65: How Individuals Obtain Health Care (Percentages may not add to 100% due to rounding)

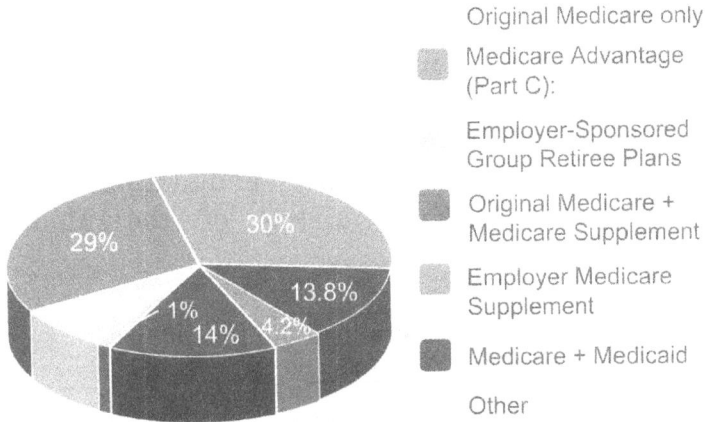

Original Medicare only

Medicare Advantage (Part C):

Employer-Sponsored Group Retiree Plans

Original Medicare + Medicare Supplement

Employer Medicare Supplement

Medicare + Medicaid

Other

Courtesy: UnitedHealthcare® Medicare Solutions
Source: Variations and Trends in Medigap Premiums, HHS, December, 2011

Another 30% of individuals on Medicare have their coverage through an employer-sponsored Group Retiree Plan. This follows 29% of individuals enrolled in one of the several types of Medicare Advantage plans. Many of these Medicare Advantage plans have prescription drug coverage included as part of their benefits. Another 13.8% of Medicare individuals purchase a Medicare Supplement/Medigap plan. Since these plans do no provide for prescription drug coverage, many of these individuals also purchase a separate Medicare Part D Prescription Drug plan (PDP). These supplement plans are offered by private insurance companies which cover most gaps in Medicare Part A and Part B, not covered by original Medicare. Another 4.2% of Medicare individuals are on an employer sponsored Medicare Supplement/Medigap plan, while 14% of Medicare consumers receive their additional coverage through Medicaid due to their low-income status. Only 1% of individuals have other public or private coverage.

In figure 2.6, using data from the Centers for Medicare & Medicaid Services Medicare Current Beneficiary 2009 Cost and Use file, the Urban Institute and Kaiser Family Foundation did an analysis of the characteristics of the Medicare population for 2012.

Figure 2.6 Characteristics of the Medicare Population, 2012

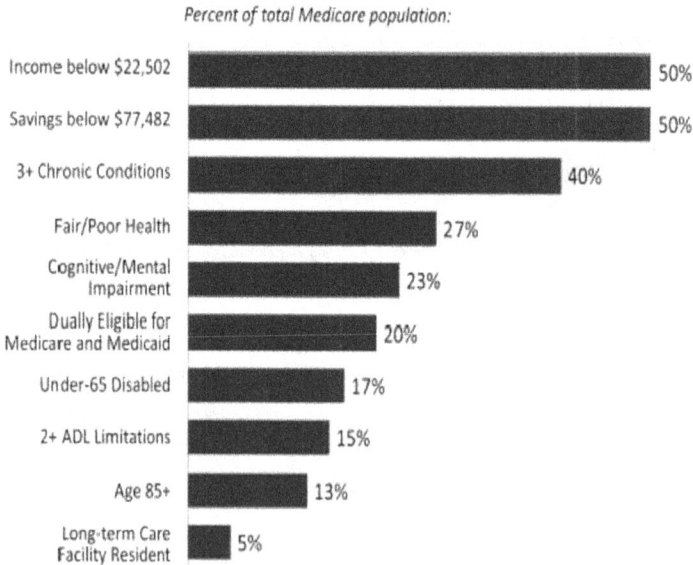

Percent of total Medicare population:

Characteristic	Percent
Income below $22,502	50%
Savings below $77,482	50%
3+ Chronic Conditions	40%
Fair/Poor Health	27%
Cognitive/Mental Impairment	23%
Dually Eligible for Medicare and Medicaid	20%
Under-65 Disabled	17%
2+ ADL Limitations	15%
Age 85+	13%
Long-term Care Facility Resident	5%

NOTE: ADL is activity of daily living.
SOURCE: Urban Institute and Kaiser Family Foundation analysis, 2012; Kaiser Family Foundation analysis of the Centers for Medicare & Medicaid Services Medicare Current Beneficiary 2009 Cost and Use file.

Source: Urban Institute and Kaiser Family Foundation Analysis, 2012

MEDICARE PAYMENT ADVISORY COMMISSION

The Medicare Payment Advisory Commission (MedPAC) is an independent Congressional agency established by the Balance Budget Act of 1997 to advise Congress on issues affecting the Medicare program. Two reports, which are issued in March and June each year, are the primary outlet for MedPAC recommendations. It also comments on reports and proposed regulations issued by the Secretary of the Department of Health and Human Services, testimony and briefings for congressional staff.

MedPAC has been reporting for years that federal payments per enrollee are higher for Medicare Advantage plans than enrollees in original fee-for-service Medicare. Health care reform was designed to phase in reductions in federal payments to Medicare Advantage plans to bring the average payment per enrollee more in line with those for original Medicare. MedPAC just recently released its March report. Highlights included:

- In 2013, MA enrollment increased by 9% to 14.5 million beneficiaries or 28% of all Medicare beneficiaries. Enrollment in HMO plans (the largest) increased 10% to nearly 10 million enrollees while local PPO plans grew 11% to 3.3 million enrollees.
- In 2013, about 68% of Medicare beneficiaries were enrolled in Part D plans, or over 35 million beneficiaries. About 64% on enrollees are in stand-alone PDPs with the remainder in

an MA-PD. 2014 premiums average about $30 across all plans.

MEDICARE SUMMARY NOTICES

If you have original Medicare every 3 months you get a Medicare Summary Notice (MSN) in the mail if you get Part A and Part B. This notice shows all the services and/or supplies that health care providers billed to Medicare during the 3 month period, what Medicare paid and what you may own the provider.

You are also able to view your Medicare claims or file an appeal online. Claims are generally available for viewing within 24 hours after processing. You will need to first register at www.MyMedicare.gov. Complete your "Initial Enrollment Questionnaire" online. This will ensure your claims are correctly paid. Once this setup is completed some of what you can do online is listed below.

- Manage personal information like medical conditions, allergies and implanted devices.
- Manage your personal drug list and pharmacy information.
- Track original Medicare claims and your Part B deductible status.
- View and order copies of your Medicare Summary Notices.
- Access to your personal health information by using Medicare's "Blue Button."

Search for, add to and manage a list of your favorite providers and access quality information about them.

MEDICARE AND OTHER HEALTH INSURANCE

When you have other insurance, there are specific rules which determine whether Medicare or your other insurance pays first.

Table 2.1 Who Pays First on Health Care Claims

If you have **retiree** insurance (insurance from your or your spouse's former employment)	Medicare pays first.
If you're 65 or older, have group health plan coverage based on your or your spouse's current employment and the employer has 20 or more employees	Your group health plan pays first.
If you're 65 or older, have group health plan coverage based on your or your spouse's current employment and the employer has less than 20 employees	Medicare pays first.
If you're under 65 and disabled, have group health plan coverage based on your or a family member's **current** employment and the employer has **100 or more employees**	Your group health plan pays first.
If you're under 65 and disabled, have group health plan coverage based on your or a family member's **current** employment, and the employer **has less than 100 employees**	Medicare pays first.
If you have Medicare because of End-Stage Renal Disease (ESRD)	Your group health plan pays the first 30 months after you become eligible to enroll in Medicare. Medicare will pay first after this period.

Source: Centers for Medicare and Medicaid Services; Medicare & You, 2014

33

There are some additional points to remember:

- The insurance that pays first (primary payer) pays up to the limits of its coverage.
- The insurance that pays second (secondary payer) only pays if there are costs the primary insurer didn't cover.
- The secondary payer (which may be Medicare) may not pay all of the uncovered costs.
- If your employer insurance is the secondary payer, you may need to enroll in Part B before your insurance will pay.

WHAT MEDICARE DOES NOT COVER

Many consumers are unaware Medicare doesn't cover all health care services and costs. On average, Medicare covers 48% of health care costs for enrollees. This leaves 52% of the health care costs being the responsibility of the enrollee. These out of pocket expenses can include the following.

- Long-term or custodial care
- Routine dental care
- Dentures
- Cosmetic surgery
- Acupuncture
- Care while travelling outside of the U.S., except under certain circumstances
- Hearing aids
- Exams for fitting hearing aids
- Vision exams and prescription eyewear
- Deductibles
- Coinsurance

- Copayments
- Supplemental insurance plans
- Routine physicals, with the exception of the one-time "Welcome to Medicare" physical exam within the first 12 months of enrolling in Medicare Part B

SUMMARIZING YOUR MEDICARE OPTIONS

Medicare health insurance options offered to consumers eligible to participate in Medicare can consist of or a combination of the following:

- Original Medicare (Part A and Part B)
- Original Medicare + Part D
- Original Medicare + Medicare Supplement
- Original Medicare + Medicare Supplement + Part D
- Medicare Advantage Part C, which may or may not include prescription drug coverage
- Original Medicare + Medicaid
- Employer-Sponsored Group Retiree Plans
- Employer Senior Supplement Group Retiree Plans

There can be penalties for not enrolling in Part A, Part B and Part D plans when you become first eligible unless you qualify for a special exemption.

EMPLOYER GROUP RETIREE PLANS

A group retiree is an individual who has retired from his/her previous employer or union and is looking for continued health care and/or prescription drug coverage through his/her previous employer or union. Health insurance companies have existing relationships with employer groups which allow them the opportunity to offer products and administer benefits for group retirees through contractual agreements and arrangements. With subsidized plans the employer contributes to the premium but with endorsed plans the employer does not pay any portion of the premiums.

Employer-provided health insurance for retirees has been declining for decades. According to Extend Health, a unit of the benefits consulting firm Towers Watson, 25% of employers who provide health insurance offer some type of financial assistance to retirees to help them with medical costs. This is down from more than 60% in the 1980s. Some companies are discontinuing their health plans for retirees and giving them a fixed amount of money to use towards their health expenses. 3M discontinued the company's traditional Medicare supplement plan in 2013 and is making contributions to retirees' health reimbursement accounts (HRAs). With establishment of the Health Insurance Marketplace and with early retirees now having guaranteed access to health insurance coverage beginning in 2014, more large employers are likely to rethink their strategy for retired former employees under age 65. Many companies may now consider dropping their coverage altogether for this former employee segment. For early retirees in that 55-64 age bracket some individuals may find their premiums could decrease through the use of the Health Insurance Marketplace.

Employees from the public sector are also not immune from these changes either. More municipalities which used to cover retiree health care expenses at 100% are now requiring formers workers to pay a monthly premium. While the premiums are usually modest, benefit coverage is also less than what it was. This trend will likely accelerate in the future with retired public employees having to contribute a larger percentage towards their health benefits through increasing premiums.

Senior supplement group retiree plans are only available through employer groups. These plans help pay for some or all of the costs not covered by original Medicare. They have similar coverage as Medicare Supplement/Medigap plans. Joining a Medicare Advantage plan may limit or end the individual's employer or union coverage for both the individual and/or family members covered by his/her group coverage plan for medical and/or prescription drugs. It's important for the individual to understand how their employer or union coverage will work with original Medicare before a decision is made about whether to enroll in a Medicare Advantage plan.

Speak with your former employer or union benefits administrator or the office that answers your health coverage questions before you make any changes to your existing health insurance coverage. Changes made could be irreversible.

MEDICARE 5-STAR QUALITY RATING SYSTEM

CMS regulates Medicare Advantage Part C and Medicare Prescription Drug Part D plans while state insurance regulators are responsible for Medicare Supplement/Medigap plans. In 2007, the CMS began rating Medicare Advantage and Prescription Drug plans sold by private healthcare insurance companies. The rating is based on a number of quality performance factors, which are discussed later. The rating system was developed and implemented in an effort to educate and allow consumers and their members to compare plans on quality and performance measures and make quality data more transparent.

Plans receive an overall quality star rating from the CMS from 1 star to 5 stars. The number of stars signifies the quality rating as illustrated below. In actual plan documents you will also see half stars incorporated into plan ratings by the CMS.

***** Excellent
****   Above Average
***   Average
**   Below Average
*   Poor

The star ratings are updated for the upcoming plan year each October and available for viewing by all Medicare consumers prior to the annual enrollment period. The plan star ratings for 2014 were released in October 2013. Star ratings for 2015 will be released in October 2014.

Each plan document will have its Star Rating included. You can also access this information on the Medicare Plan Finder for both Medicare Advantage and Medicare Prescription Drug plans. Go to www.medicare.gov/find-a-plan/questions/home.aspx. Enter your zip code then click on the "Find Plans" button. If you're unsure what to enter, select "I don't know" option. Next, click on "Continue to Plan Results." If you want to skip the drug component, select "I don't want to add drugs now." Follow the remainder of the steps. The Star Ratings will be in the column titled "Overall Plan Ratings."

The Affordable Care Act and Star Ratings

The passage of the Affordable Care Act (ACA) added some weight to the star ratings by tying federal reimbursement rates for insurance carriers administering Medicare Advantage plans, by awarding bonus payments and larger rebates to plans which achieve higher quality ratings. In 2010, a bonus payment for plans receiving 4 or more stars was introduced. Then in 2012, the CMS launched a 3-year demonstration project, until 2015, which extended these bonuses to plans which score 3 or more stars. The CMS demonstration project increases the amount of bonus payments and scales them to the plan's star ratings. The higher the rating the larger the bonus the insurer receives. The bonuses are designed to create larger, more rapid quality improvements across the Medicare program and to recognize individual health care plans for their results. Plans which have a 5-star rating will be able to enroll members throughout the year and will also receive a 10% quality bonus. Starting in 2015, the CMS quality bonuses will only be awarded to plans with either a 4-star or higher rating.

These bonus payments must be used by plan sponsors to enhance benefits and keep costs down. This can include offering vision care or lowering cost sharing. These bonuses can potentially give plans a competitive advantage allowing them to offer more attractive benefit packages. The health insurers are placing a significant emphasis on improving their star ratings. For those that maintain less than 3 stars on their various plans, these insurers are likely to see significant cuts in their funding from Medicare. From now until 2017, the insurer landscape is probably going to change with fewer carriers left offering Medicare Advantage plans.

In 2012, the CMS began their "Consistent Poor Performer Notice" campaign. Medicare mails this notice to members of Medicare Advantage and Prescription Drug plans who are enrolled in plans that have had an overall star rating of "poor" or "below average" for at least the last three years. The notice is usually mailed in late October after current Star Ratings are released. The notice is designed to encourage members to use the AEP as an opportunity to review other plans available in their area and consider enrolling in a plan with a higher star rating. In February 2014, the CMS is conducting another mailing to Medicare plan members with a January 1, 2014 effective date who have recently enrolled in a low performing plan. They will have a special one-time SEP to enroll in a plan rated 3-Stars or higher.

5 Star Rated Plans

After December 8, 2011, members were allowed to switch to a plan which has an overall 5-star rating at any time during the year. However, you can only switch to a 5-star plan once each year. An individual can switch from December 8 until November 30 of the following year. If they switch to a 5-star plan, the individual must remain in the plan through the plan year unless they qualify for a different SEP. For 2014, the National Council on Aging reported there were 19

Medicare contracts which received a five-star rating. There are many service areas and even states with no five-star rated plans so there is a chance you may not have access to one.

Performance and Quality Ratings

Medicare measures how well health and prescription drug plans perform on more than 50 items, which are then grouped into different categories.

Medicare Advantage Plans

For plans covering health services the overall score for quality of those services covers 36 different topics in 5 categories. These 5 categories are:

- Staying Healthy: Screening, Tests and Vaccines.
- Managing Chronic Long-Term Conditions.
- Health Plan Responsiveness and Care.
- Member Complaints, Problems Getting Service and Choosing to Leave the Plan.
- Health Plan Telephone Customer Service.

Medicare Prescription Drug Plans

For plans covering drug services the overall score for quality of those services covers 17 different topics in 4 categories. These 4 categories are:

- Drug Plan Customer Service.
- Member Complaints, Problems Getting Service and Choosing to Leave the Plan.
- Member Experience with Drug Plan.

- Drug Pricing and Patient Safety.

For plans covering both, health and drug services, the overall score for quality of those services covers all 53 topics from the 9 categories listed above.

Where does the information for the overall plan ratings come from? For quality of health services the information comes from sources which include:

- Member surveys done by Medicare.
- Information from clinicians.
- Information submitted by the plans.
- Results obtained from Medicare's regular monitoring activities.

For quality of drug services the information comes from sources which include:

- Results obtained from Medicare's regular monitoring activities.
- Reviews of billing and other information that plans submit to Medicare.
- Member surveys done by Medicare.

Members may lose their prescription drug coverage if they move from a MA-PD plan which has drug coverage to a MA plan that does not. You may have to wait until the next annual enrollment period to obtain drug coverage and you may have to pay a Late Enrollment Penalty also.

While these star ratings have been a hot topic within the Medicare insurance industry, in an October 2011 research report from Kaiser Permanente, many consumers have a low awareness of the star rating system and rarely use it in choosing a health plan. In their study only 18% of Medicare eligible members were familiar with Medicare's rating system and just 2% knew their own health plan rating. The bottom line for consumers is they should select plans which provide the best coverage of health care and prescription drugs they need while fitting within their health care budget.

SOME FUTURE PRESPECTIVE ON MEDICARE

If you're currently enroll in original Medicare, have Medicare Advantage or Medicare Supplement/Medigap or have health coverage through a retiree employer-sponsored health plan there is nothing for you to worry about regarding the new health care law. You have creditable health coverage and will not face a penalty.

The ACA significantly expanded several preventive health measures for Medicare recipients. It also reduces or eliminates out-of-pocket costs for a variety of life-saving screenings. Beneficiaries once had to pay coinsurance amounts of 20% for many preventive services. Beneficiaries used to receive a one-time only "Welcome to Medicare" visit with their primary care physician (PCP) at no cost. Now beneficiaries can receive an annual wellness visit with their PCP at no out-of-pocket expense. This is not a full physical but involves a comprehensive health risk assessment. Medicare now also covers screenings for cancer, depression, obesity, diabetes and other chronic illnesses. It also extends to alcohol counseling, smoking cessation and nutritional consultations. For more information about preventive service Medicare has a *"Guide to Medicare's Preventive Services"* available at www.medicare.gov/Pubs/pdf/10110.pdf.

The ACA also mandates greater prescription drug coverage on Medicare Part D Prescription Drug plans. Prior to the ACA enactment beneficiaries had to pay 100% of drug costs if they reached the coverage gap or donut hole as it is also called. Since 2011 beneficiaries have been paying a reduced amount each year. For 2014, beneficiaries will pay 47.5% for brand-name prescriptions and 72% for generic prescriptions. The ACA has been gradually closing this coverage gap each year since 2010, when in 2020, both of these amounts will be reduced to and remain at 25% for both.

Obamacare cuts government funding to Medicare by $716 billion between 2013 and 2022, in order to pay for part of the law's $1.9 trillion in new health care spending for younger individuals over the same time frame. Much of this comes from new measures to reduce fraudulent spending. Entitlement programs will come under greater scrutiny in years to come. While health care technology innovation is very rich in this country it comes with a price; a price which entitlement programs may just not want to cover regardless of patient benefits and outcomes. There is only so much money to go around. In the economic environment we're in, Medicare and Medicaid are meant to be backstop programs. They're not intended to get you anything and everything. If the federal government perseveres and accomplishes its goal and health care reforms become a success, a future presidential administration might use the Health Insurance Marketplace as an effective replacement for the single-payer health care entitlement programs of

Medicare and Medicaid, which would simply be absorbed within the Health Insurance Marketplace.

2014 - WHAT'S NEW AND IMPORTANT

The CMS recently said health care reform efforts are eliciting significant out-of-pocket savings for Medicare beneficiaries. As a result, there will be no premium or deductible increases for Part B coverage in 2014.

Preventive Care Benefits

More preventive services are covered for 2014. Coverage will now include depression screenings, screenings, counseling for alcohol misuse and obesity and behavioral therapy for cardiovascular disease.

Premium for Part A

If required to pay a premium for Part A coverage, it will decrease $15 to $426, down from $441 in 2013.

Deductible for Part A

Deductibles will increase $32 to $1,216, up from $1,184 in 2013.

Premium for Part B

Premiums remain the same at $104.90 a month. By law, the standard Part B premium represents roughly one-fourth of the average cost for beneficiaries aged 65 and over plus a contingency margin to provide for possible variations between actual and projected costs.

Deductible for Part B

The deductible will also stay the same at $147 in 2014.

Monthly Premium for Part D

Monthly premium will increase 4% to $32.42, up from $31.17 in 2013.

Initial Deductible for Part D

Beneficiaries will see costs decrease for prescription drug coverage again. Initial deductible will decrease by $15 to $310 in 2014.

Initial Coverage Limit for Part D

The initial coverage limit will decrease from $2,970 in 2013 to $2,850 in 2014, a decrease of $120.

Out-of-Pocket Threshold for Part D

The out-of-pocket threshold will decrease from $4,790 in 2013 to $4,550 in 2014.

Help in the Prescription Drug Coverage Gap

If you reach the coverage gap (donut hole) in your Medicare prescription drug coverage (Part D), you will pay only 47.5% for covered brand-name prescription drugs and 72% for generic drugs.

Copayments in Catastrophic Coverage

Once a beneficiary reaches catastrophic coverage, generic/preferred prescriptions will cost $2.55, down from $2.65 in 2013 while brand name prescriptions will cost $6.35 in 2014, down from $6.60 in 2013. The 5% coinsurance, whichever is greater still applies.

Income Related Adjustments

Individuals with Medicare, who report 2012 income above $85,000 a year and those filing jointly, with incomes of $170,000, are legally responsible to cover a larger portion of the cost of their coverage. These premium adjustments range from $42.00 to $230.80 a month for Medicare Part B.

Doc Fix

In March 2014, the House passed a 12 month "Doc Fix" by voice vote. The bill avoids a 24% reduction in payment for doctors who treat Medicare patients.

Outlook for 2015

The CMS in its proposed 2015 draft call letter and advance rate notice has proposed a 5.9% cut to Medicare Advantage (MA). In a recent Oliver Wyman report, if the changes proposed by CMS are implemented, the program would be hit by a double-digit cut over just a two year period resulting in increased costs, reduced benefits and fewer coverage options for seniors. Final MA payment rates will be announced on April 7, 2014 by the CMS.

"It is time that we provide clarity for our seniors, informing them of the services available that will lower the costs of their prescription drugs and strengthen the overall integrity of the Medicare entitlement"

Olympia Snowe
Republican U.S. Senator – Maine
First Lady of Maine
Republican U.S. House of Representatives -Maine's
2nd Congressional District
Maine Senate
Maine House of Representatives

CHAPTER THREE

MEDICARE TERMINOLOGY

Some writers will place a terminology section at the end of their book in the appendix or glossary. As you read if there is a term you don't understand you've got to flip to the back of the book to see if the word and its definition are included there. I opted to include a terminology section as a separate chapter because I believe if you understand the key terminology used in navigating the Medicare process it will be easier for you to more quickly understand the various programs, attributes and costs you might incur and which may be best suited to your health care needs.

The good thing is if you have health insurance through an employer sponsored plan or individually on your own many of these terms will share the same meaning. If that's the case this chapter will simply serve as a review for you. Many of the terms discussed here will again be defined in subsequent chapters to follow. The definitions are in alphabetical order.

ANOC: If you're already a member of a Medicare plan, offered by a health insurance company, this is the Annual Notice of Change (ANOC) letter you will receive by September 30th each year. This letter informs you of any changes being made to your plan for the upcoming plan year.

Assignment: This is an agreement by your physician or other medical supplier to be paid directly by Medicare. With assignment your physician or supplier agrees to accept the payment Medicare approves for the service or supply and will not bill you for any more than the Medicare deductible and any coinsurance, if applicable.

Benefit Period: How original Medicare measures your use of hospital and skilled nursing facility (SNF) services. A benefit period begins the day you're admitted as an inpatient in a hospital or skilled nursing facility. The benefit period ends when you haven't received any inpatient hospital care or skilled care in an SNF for 60 days in a row.

Coinsurance: This is the amount you may be required to pay as your share of the costs for medical services and treatments after you pay any deductibles. Coinsurance is usually a percentage of the cost such as 20%. Since this is a percentage this will be a variable dollar amount as opposed to a fixed amount.

Copayment: This is the amount you may be required to pay as your share of the cost for a medical service or supply such as a physician's visit, hospital outpatient visit or a prescription. Copayments are usually a fixed dollar cost such as $10 or $20 for a physician's visit.

Critical Access Hospital: This is a small facility which provides outpatient, as well as inpatient services on a limited basis, to people in rural areas.

Creditable Prescription Drug Coverage: Prescription drug coverage, which you have through an employer or union that's expected to pay, on average, at least as much as Medicare's standard prescription drug coverage.

Custodial Care: This is non-skilled personal care, such as help with activities of daily living like bathing, dressing, eating, getting in or out of a bed or chair, moving around and using the bathroom.

Deductible: This is the amount you must pay for health care needs or prescription drugs before original Medicare, your prescription drug plan or other insurance you may have begins to pay.

Excess Charge: If you are enrolled in original Medicare and your physician or medical supplier is legally permitted to charge for services which, are higher than the Medicare-approved amount, this difference is called an excess charge. You may be responsible for the additional amount. Always ask your physician if they bill excess charges.

Extra Help: A Medicare program to assist individuals with limited income and resources pay Medicare prescription drug plan costs, such as premiums, deductibles and coinsurance.

Formulary: This is a list of prescription drugs covered by a prescription drug plan or other insurance plan offering prescription drug benefits.

Guaranteed Issue Rights: These are rights you have in certain situations when health insurance companies are required by law to sell or offer you a policy. They can't deny you a policy or place conditions on a policy such as pre-existing conditions or charge you more for a policy because of past or present health conditions. These "rights" are usually seen in a Medicare Supplement/Medigap type plan.

Guaranteed Renewable Policy: An insurance policy cannot be terminated by the insurance company unless you make untrue statements on the application, commit fraud or don't pay your premiums.

Inpatient Rehabilitation Facility: This is a hospital or part of a hospital which provides an intensive rehabilitation program to inpatients.

Institution: This is a facility which provides short term or long term care, such as a nursing home, skilled nursing facility (SNF) or rehabilitation hospital. Private residences, such as an assisted living facility or group home aren't considered institutions for this purpose.

Lifetime Reserve Days: In original Medicare these are additional days that Medicare will pay for when you're in the hospital for more than 90 days. You have a total of 60 reserve days that can be used during your lifetime.

Long Term Care (LTC): A variety of services which assist individuals with their medical and non-medical needs over a period of time. LTC can be provided for at home, in the community or in various types of facilities including nursing homes and assisted living facilities. Most LTC is custodial care which Medicare typically doesn't cover.

Medical Underwriting: The process an insurance company uses to determine, based on your medical history, whether or not to take your application for insurance, add a waiting period for pre-existing conditions (if your state law allows it) and how much to charge you for insurance.

Medically Necessary: Services or supplies which are needed for the diagnosis or treatment of your medical condition and meet accepted standards of medical practice.

Medicare-Approved Amount: With original Medicare this is the amount a physician or medical supplier that accepts assignment can be paid. It may less than the actual amount which the physician or medical supplier charges non-Medicare patients.

Pre-existing Condition: It is a health issue which you currently have and are being treated for or you previously had and was treated under a physician's care. Beginning in 2014, you cannot be denied health insurance coverage for any pre-existing condition.

Premium: The periodic payment you make either, monthly or quarterly to Medicare, an insurance company or health care plan for health care or prescription drug coverage. Failure to pay your premiums could result in loss of coverage.

Preventive Services: Health care to prevent illness or detect illness at an early stage when treatment is likely to work best.

Primary Care Physician (PCP): This is the physician you see first for most health problems. The PCP will coordinate will other physicians, if needed, to develop treatment plans including referrals to medical specialists. In many Medicare Advantage plans you must see your PCP before you see any other health care providers.

Quality Improvement Organization (QIO): A group of practicing physicians and other health care experts paid by the Federal government to check and improve the care given to people with Medicare.

Referral: A written order from your PCP for you to see a specialist or to get specific medical services.

Service Area: A geographic area where a health insurance plan accepts members, if it limits membership based on where individuals live.

CHAPTER FOUR

ENROLLMENT & DISENROLLMENT PERIODS

As opposed to covering the enrollment and disenrollment periods for each plan in their specific chapter, we're going to cover these time periods for these various Medicare plans in the same chapter. Each plan's specific features and benefits will then be covered in subsequent chapters.

ELIGIBILITY

Eligibility for original Medicare is very straight forward. In general, you can participate if:

- You or your spouse worked for at least 10 years (40 quarters) in Medicare-covered employment and you are 65 years of age or older and have been legal residents of the United States for at least 5 years.

- Individuals under the age of 65 with certain disabilities may also be eligible if they have received Social Security Disability Insurance (SSDI) benefits for at least 24 months.
- Individuals of any age with End Stage Renal Disease (permanent kidney failure requiring dialysis or transplant).

ENROLLMENT BASICS

The enrollment period in Medicare is based on whether you're discussing Medicare Part A and Part B, Medicare Advantage Part C, Medicare Prescription Drug Part D or Medicare Supplement/Medigap plans.

1. MEDICARE PART A and PART B

Enrollment for Part A and/or Part B can occur in one of four ways.

1. Under 65 and Already Enrolled in Social Security or the Railroad Retirement Board

If you are currently receiving benefits from Social Security Administration (SSA) or the Railroad Retirement Board (RRB), you will be automatically enrolled in Medicare Part A and Part B. Part A will be premium-free unless you meet certain circumstances to be discussed later while Part B is a voluntary program which will require a monthly premium.

Medicare will mail you a Medicare card and general information before the date you become eligible. Should you decide you don't want to keep Part B you must follow the instructions you get when you receive your Medicare card to let Medicare know that you don't want to keep Part B. Otherwise, you will be charged the Part B premium. These premiums will be deducted directly from your existing monthly Social Security or Railroad Retirement benefits. Your benefits will start the first day of the month you turn age 65.

If you're getting disability benefits from Social Security or certain disability benefits from RRB, benefits will start the first day of the 25th month after your disability benefits began. Beware of the fact that should you decide you don't want Part B when you're eligible, you may have to pay a penalty to get it later.

2. Turning Age 65 - Initial Enrollment Period

If you're not currently receiving either Social Security or RRB benefits then you will have to enroll in order to receive Medicare benefits. About 3 months before you're eligible for Medicare you can apply by either making an appointment at your nearest Social Security office or by going online at www.socialsecurity.gov and selecting "Apply Online for Medicare only." In addition, there's a short video you can access which is about 1 minute in length that discusses the Medicare online enrollment process at http://www.socialsecurity.gov/multimedia/video/iClaim _English_Retirement_Page/iClaim_English_Retiremen t_Page.mp4. Social Security estimates you can complete the application process in between 10 and 30 minutes, depending on the number of questions you need to answer. You can save your application as you go so you can take a break at any time. Use the "More Info" links if you need more information. Answer the questions about current benefits you may be receiving, such as Medicaid or other health insurance and select "Submit Now" to send your application electronically to Social Security. You will see a receipt on the screen which you can print and keep for your records. You also will get an application number that you can use to check the status of your application. Social Security will review your application and contact you if there is a need for clarification about your answers or if there is a need to see any documents. Your application will be processed and a letter mail to you about their decision.

There are several advantages in applying for Medicare online. Some of these advantages include:

- Start your application immediately. You do not have to wait for an appointment.
- Apply from the comfort of your home or any computer.
- Avoid a trip to the Social Security office saving you time and money.
- Don't have to complete the application in one sitting. If you want to take a break you can stop working on the application. Restart again without losing any of the information you entered.

You can sign up for Medicare when you become first eligible during what is called the Initial Enrollment Period (IEP). This is a 7-month period that begins 3 months before the month you turn 65, the month you turn 65 and 3 months after the month you turn 65. If this seems confusing, table 4.1 below should clarify the enrollment period.

Table 4.1 Medicare Initial Enrollment Timetable

3 months before the month you turn 65	2 months before the month you turn 65	1 month before the month you turn 65	The month you turn 65	1 month after the month you turn 65	2 months after the month you turn 65	3 months after the month you turn 65
Sign up early to avoid a delay in coverage. To get Part A and/or Part B the month you turn 65, you must sign up during the first 3 months before the month you turn 65.			If you wait until the last 4 months of your Initial Enrollment Period to sign up for Part and/or Part B, your coverage will be delayed.			

Source: Medicare

If you enroll for Medicare during the **first three months of your IEP** your coverage start date will depend on your birthday. There are two options:

- If your birthday ISN'T the first day of the month, coverage starts the first day of your birthday month. For example, Tom's birthday is June 21st. If he enrolls in March, April or May, his coverage will start June 1st.
- If your birthday IS on the first day of the month, your coverage will start the first day of the

month prior to your birth month. For example, Linda's birthday is May 1st. If she enrolls in January, February or March, her coverage will start on April 1st. To use the chart above correctly, use the month before her birthday as the month you turn 65.

Depending on your health insurance coverage before turning 65, there is a definite advantage to enrolling before your birth month.

If you enroll in Medicare the month you turn 65 or during the next three months of your IEP your coverage start date will be delayed. Table 4.2 below illustrates this delay in coverage.

Table 4.2 IEP For Birth Month and Later Medicare Coverage Start Delay

If you enroll in this month of your Initial Enrollment Period	Your Medicare coverage starts
The month you turn 65	1 month after enrollment
1 month after you turn 65	2 months after enrollment
2 months after you turn 65	3 months after enrollment
3 months after you turn 65	3 months after enrollment

Courtesy: Medicare

3. General Enrollment Period

If you didn't enroll for Medicare during your IEP you can sign up from January 1 – March 31 each year during the General Enrollment Period (GEP). However, your coverage will not begin until July 1st. You may also have to pay a higher premium because of the late enrollment after your IEP.

For example, Judy turns 65 in June 2013. Her IEP would be from March 2013 through September 2013. However, Judy doesn't enroll during this period. She will now have to wait for the GEP. Judy enrolls in January 2014. Coverage will not begin until July 1, 2014.

4. Special Enrollment Period

If you didn't enroll for Medicare during your IEP because you were covered under an employer-sponsored health insurance plan, based on current employment, you qualify for a Special Enrollment Period (SEP). You can enroll in Medicare anytime that you or your spouse (or family member if you're disabled) are working and you're covered by a group health plan through the employer based on that work or **during the 8-month period that begins the month after the employment ends or the group health plan coverage ends**, whichever happens first.

COBRA and retiree health plans are not considered coverage based on current employment. You're not eligible for an SEP when that coverage ends. To avoid paying a higher premium, enroll for Medicare when you're first eligible. If you have ESRD this enrollment period doesn't apply to you. If you're a volunteer serving in a foreign country you may qualify for an SEP also.

Premium Penalties for Late Enrollments

If you don't enroll in Medicare during your IEP you may have to pay a penalty unless you're eligible for a SEP. The penalty may apply both to Part A and Part B.

For Part A the penalty is equal to 10% of the premium. This penalty applies no matter how long you delay enrollment and the penalty needs to be paid for twice the number of years you could have had Part A coverage. For example, Dave delayed his enrollment for three years. Dave must pay the 10% penalty amount for six years before the penalty is removed.

For Part B the penalty calculation is different and more onerous. If you don't enroll for Part B when you're first eligible you will not only have to pay the 10% premium penalty but pay the 10% for **each 12-month period you delay** unless you're eligible for an SEP. In addition, you will have to **pay this penalty every month** for as long as you have Part B coverage. If you're enrolled in Part B because of a disability and you're under 65 and paying the penalty, once you turn 65 you no longer have to pay this penalty.

For example, Ken's IEP ended September 30, 2008. He waited until the 2011 GEP (1/01-3/31) and enrolled in Part B in March 2011. Thus, Ken waited a total of 30 months before he enrolled in Part B. Since this time period includes two full 12-month periods (24 months), Ken's Part B premium penalty is 20% (10% x 2) for as long as he is enrolled in Part B coverage. If Ken waited another 6 months before enrolling, he would have waited a total of 36 months. Since this now includes three full 12-month periods, his premium penalty would be 30% for as long as he is enrolled in Part B.

Your New Medicare Card

Once your application is approved your red, white and blue Medicare card will be mailed to you. Keep your card in safe place and welcome to the Medicare health insurance program.

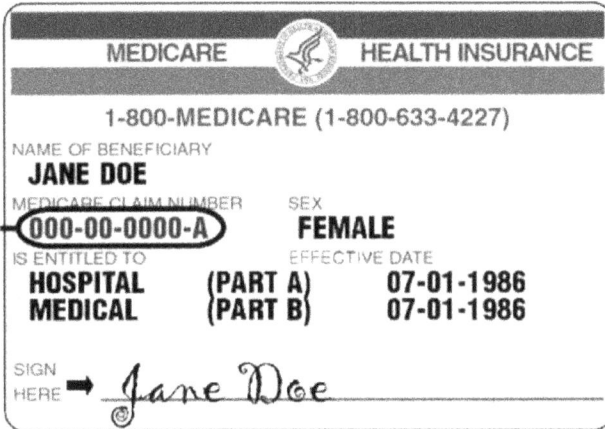

2. MEDICARE ADVANTAGE (MA) PART C PLANS

Individuals can join a Medicare Advantage plan if they meet the following conditions.

- You must be entitled to and enrolled in Medicare Part A **and** Part B.
- The beneficiary of the plan must permanently reside in the MA plan's service area, which is usually county-based. Also the beneficiary must be able to make an informed decision.
- In most cases if you have End-Stage Renal Disease (ESRD) you can't join a Medicare Advantage plan.

As with Medicare Part A and Part B, there are specific times you can enroll for a MA plan or make changes to the coverage you already have.

1. Initial Enrollment Period

If you're first eligible for Medicare because you turned 65, the period for enrollment in MA plans is exactly the same as the Initial Enrollment Period (IEP) for Medicare Part A and Part B. There is a 7-month period that starts 3 months before the month you turn 65, the month you turn 65 and ends 3 months after the month you turn 65.

If you're first eligible for Medicare because you're disabled and under 65, the enrollment period begins during the 7-month period that starts 3 months before your 25th month of disability, includes the 25th month of disability and ends 3 months after your 25th month of disability. For example, if the 25th month after you became disabled was October 2012, three months before would include July, August and September and 3 months after would include November, December and January 2013.

If you're already eligible for Medicare because of a disability and you turn 65, it is the same IEP as discussed at the beginning of this section. However, if you sign up for an MA plan during this period you have the option to drop that MA plan at any time during the next twelve months and go back to original Medicare Part A and Part B if you do not like the Medicare Advantage plan.

2. General Enrollment Period

If you already have Medicare Part A and you enroll in Part B during the General Enrollment Period (GEP) from January 1st through March 31st, you can enroll for a MA plan with or without prescription drug coverage between April 1st and June 30th of the same year. Coverage will begin on July 1st of the same year.

3. Medicare Advantage Annual Enrollment Period, also called Open Enrollment Period

Each year members have two separate enrollment periods to make changes to their Medicare Advantage coverage for the upcoming plan year.

1. October 15 – December 7

Changes made during this period will take effect on January 1st. During this period you can do the following:

- Change from original Medicare to a Medicare Advantage plan.
- Change from a Medicare Advantage plan back to original Medicare.
- Switch from one Medicare Advantage plan to another Medicare Advantage plan.
- Switch from a Medicare Advantage plan that doesn't offer drug coverage to a Medicare Advantage plan that offers drug coverage.
- Switch from a Medicare Advantage plan that offers drug coverage to a Medicare Advantage plan that doesn't offer drug coverage.

2. January 1 – February 14

This is a 45 day period when a member can disenroll from their current MA plan if they choose. During this period you can do the following:

- If you're in a Medicare Advantage plan you can leave your plan and switch to original Medicare. Your original Medicare coverage will begin the first day of the following month.
- If you switch to original Medicare during this period you have until February 14 to also join a Medicare Prescription Drug plan to add drug coverage. Your prescription drug coverage will begin the first day of the month after the plan gets your enrollment form.

During this period, you CAN'T do the following:

- Switch from original Medicare to a Medicare Advantage plan.
- Switch from one Medicare Advantage plan to another Medicare Advantage plan.

4. Special Enrollment Period

Changes can be made to your Medicare Advantage plan when certain events happen in your life. These would include changes in where you live, changes that cause you to lose your current coverage, changes in your plan's contract with Medicare or changes due to other special circumstances. Rules about when you can make these changes and the type of changes you can make are different for each Special Enrollment Period (SEP).

3. MEDICARE PRESCRIPTION DRUG PART D PLANS

Medicare offers prescription drug coverage to individuals with Medicare. To join a Medicare Part D plan the individual must have Medicare Part A **and/or** Part B. In most cases you can only join a Medicare Part D plan at certain times during the year.

1. Initial Enrollment Period

You're first eligible for Medicare because you turned 65. The period for enrollment in Medicare Part D Prescription Drug plan is exactly the same as the Initial Enrollment Period (IEP) for Medicare Part A and Part B. There is a 7-month period that starts 3 months before the month you turn 65, the month you turn 65 and ends 3 months after the month you turn 65.

If you're newly eligible for Medicare because you're disabled and under 65, the enrollment period begins during the 7-month period that starts 3 months before your 25th month of disability, includes the 25th month of disability and ends 3 months after your 25th month of disability. For example, if the 25th month after you became disabled was October 2012, three months before would include July, August and September and 3 months after would include November, December and January 2013. If you're already eligible for Medicare because of a disability and you turn 65 it is the same IEP as earlier discussed.

2. General Enrollment Period

If you don't have Medicare Part A coverage and you enroll in Medicare Part B during the General Enrollment Period (GEP) from January 1st through March 31st, the earliest you can enroll in a Medicare Part D plan will be between April 1st and June 30th of the same year. Coverage in the Medicare Part D plan will start on July 1st of the same year.

3. Medicare Prescription Drug Open Enrollment Period

Each year members have two separate enrollment periods to make changes to their Medicare Prescription Part D Drug coverage for the upcoming plan year.

1. October 15 – December 7

Changes made during this period take effect on January 1st. During this period you can do the following:

- Switch from a Medicare Advantage plan that doesn't offer drug coverage to a Medicare Advantage plan that offers drug coverage.
- Switch from a Medicare Advantage plan that offers drug coverage to a Medicare Advantage plan that doesn't offer coverage.
- Join a Medicare Prescription Drug plan (PDP).
- Switch from one Medicare PDP to another Medicare PDP.
- Drop your Medicare prescription drug coverage completely.

2. January 1 – February 14

During this period you can do the following:

- If you switch to original Medicare during this period, you will have until February 14 to also join a Medicare Prescription Part D Drug plan to add drug coverage. Your prescription drug coverage will begin the first day of the month after the plan gets your enrollment form.

Note: During this period, you CAN'T do the following:

- Switch from one Medicare Prescription Part D Drug plan to another.
- Join, switch, or drop a Medicare Medical Savings Account Plan.

4. Special Enrollment Period (SEP)

Changes can be made to your Medicare Prescription Part D Drug plan when certain events happen in your life. These include changes in where you live, changes that cause you to lose your current coverage, changes in your plan's contract with Medicare or changes due to other special circumstances. Rules about when you can make these changes and the type of changes you can make are different for each Special Enrollment Period (SEP).

Premium Penalties for Late Enrollments

If an individual doesn't enroll during their initial eligibility period, a penalty may be applied. Penalties begin following 63 continuous days after the individual's initial enrollment period or loss of creditable coverage occurs. The late enrollment penalty is calculated by multiplying 1% of the 2014 "national base beneficiary premium" of $32.42 times the number of full, uncovered months you were eligible but didn't join a Medicare Prescription Drug Plan. This number can change annually. This amount is added to your monthly premium and is a Medicare requirement which cannot be waived or changed by the plan unless the individual qualifies for an exception. The penalty is paid as long as the individual is enrolled in any Medicare Prescription Drug Plan. Individuals who receive a low-income subsidy are not assessed a late enrollment penalty.

4. MEDICARE SUPPLEMENT/MEDIGAP PLANS

You must be enrolled in Medicare Part A **and** Part B in order to purchase a Medicare Supplement/Medigap plan. These plans are designed to fill in the coverage gaps which original Medicare doesn't cover. Medicare Supplement/Medigap plans are sold by private health insurance companies. They are also called Med Supp plans.

The initial Open Enrollment Period (OEP) is one-time only. By federal law, this 6-month period gives you guaranteed acceptance, regardless of your health status, to buy any Med Supp policy that is sold in your state. The period begins with the first day of the month in which you are both age 65 or older and enrolled in Medicare Part B. There is no medical underwriting. Some plans may have a waiting period for pre-existing conditions. These plans will be covered in detail in Chapter 9. Once this period starts it can't be delayed or changed. Some states may have additional open enrollment rights under state law.

If you apply for coverage after your Med Supp OEP ends, there is no guarantee that an insurance company will sell you a policy if you don't meet the medical underwriting requirements for eligibility. There are limited situations where an insurance company can't refuse to sell you a Med Supp/Medigap policy. These specific situations are listed in the CMS guide, *2013, Choosing a Medigap Policy,* pages 22-23.

DISENROLLMENT BASICS

CMS sets the conditions and steps required which a health plan must take for required involuntary disenrollment and optional involuntary enrollment.

Medicare Advantage Disenrollment Period (MA-DP)

Plan members have an annual opportunity to dis-enroll from any MA plan and return to original Medicare between January 1 and February 14 of every year. The effective date of a disenrollment request made using the MA-DP will be the first month following receipt of the disenrollment request. For example, Pat made a request in February to disenroll from his MA plan. His disenrollment will be effective March 1st.

The MA-DP does not provide an opportunity to join or switch MA plans. Regardless of whether your MA plan had prescription drug coverage, you are eligible for a coordinating Medicare Prescription Part D SEP to enroll in a PDP. If you're enrolled in an MA-PFFS plan you must request disenrollment from the PFFS plan in order to be eligible for this SEP as enrollment in a PDP will not result in automatic disenrollment from the MA-PFFS.

Voluntary Disenrollment

An individual may request disenrollment from an MA plan only during one of the election periods. You may disenroll by:

- Enrolling in another plan during a valid enrollment period.
- Giving or faxing a signed written notice to the MA organization or through his/her employer or union.
- Submitting a request via the internet to the MA organization if the option is offered.
- Calling 1-800-MEDICARE.

Required Involuntary Disenrollment

The MA organization must disenroll a member from an MA plan in the following cases:

- A change in residence makes the individual ineligible to remain enrolled.
- You become incarcerated.
- You lose entitlement to either Medicare Part A or Medicare Part B.
- A SNP member loses special needs status and does not reestablish SNP eligibility prior to the expiration of the period of deemed continued eligibility.
- You die.

- The MA organization's contract is terminated or the MA organization reduces its service area to exclude the member.

Optional Involuntary Disenrollment

An MA organization may disenroll a member from its MA plan it offers if:

- Premiums, if required, are not paid on a timely basis.
- The member engages in disruptive behavior.
- The member provides fraudulent information on the enrollment application.

Notice Requirements for Involuntary Disenrollment

In a situation where the MA organization disenrolls the member involuntary, the MA organization must send notice of the upcoming disenrollment which meets the following requirements:

- Advises the member the MA organization is planning to disenroll and why such action is occurring.
- Provides the effective date of termination.
- Includes an explanation of the member's right to a hearing under the MA organization's Grievance procedures.

Notices must be mailed to the member before submission of the disenrollment transaction to the CMS.

REVIEW YOUR CURRENT MEDICARE PLAN ANNUALLY

Your health situation can change from one year to the next as well as your financial circumstances. Medicare premiums and benefit costs can change from year to year also. If you are already enrolled in a private insurance Medicare health plan or a Medicare Prescription Part D Drug plan, your plan sponsor can **change how much it costs and what benefits are covered each year.** Even if your plans' costs and benefit coverage remain the same, your health and/or finances may have changed during the year. The physicians and/or hospitals you use can also change. Your Medicare health insurance provider could eliminate your plan altogether. That's why it's important to do an annual Medicare plan review each fall.

If you're currently enrolled in a Medicare Advantage or Medicare Prescription Part D Drug plan, each fall you will receive your ANOC (Annual Notice of Change) letter from your plan sponsor. You should receive it by September 30th. This letter will describe the changes which will occur in your plan effective January 1st of the coming year. These changes could include plan costs and benefits covered. Make sure you read and understand the contents of this letter.

After you have read your ANOC letter, it's a good idea to review your specific plan to make sure it will continue to meet your needs for the following year. Are there any changes to costs you pay, benefits you currently use, prescription drugs you use, the pharmacy you use, the physicians you go to or the hospitals where you have medical procedures done? If

74

you're satisfied that your current plan will meet your needs for next year you don't need to do anything.

Even if you are satisfied with your plan you should remain engaged in the Medicare process each year as to what is occurring and changing within the Medicare arena. Why? You may be able to find another plan which costs less money and still provides you with the same benefits and coverage that you currently have. Who doesn't like to save a little money now and then? Or you may be able to find additional benefits which you can take advantage of.

In a survey of 1,100 individuals over the age of 65, commissioned by Express Scripts in August 2013, the survey found a high degree of confusion about Medicare without even getting into the *Affordable Care Act* (ACA). Among the key findings from the survey were:

- Of those 65 and older, 26% didn't know how to choose a Medicare plan.
- Of those with a current plan, 31% indicated they would rather stay with their current plan rather than deal with finding a better one.
- Sixty-five percent didn't know the Open Enrollment Period for Medicare begins in October.
- Seventy-five percent didn't know that as a result of the passage of ACA the coverage gap for prescription drugs, also known as the donut hole, will completely disappear by 2020.

In a recent survey conducted by Humana those individuals which do evaluate their options, on average, spend 22 hours reading brochures, talking to friends and gathering information. Twenty-nine percent of women and 23% of men said they were overwhelmed by the selection process. What sources of information do individuals rely on when choosing Medicare coverage? Humana's survey uncovered the following:

- Booklet from Medicare – 56%
- Help from friends – 30%
- Sales brochure from insurance company – 25%
- Help from spouse – 25%
- Sales agent guidance – 21%
- News websites or the internet – 18%
- Newspapers – 16%
- Help from colleagues – 16%
- Help from family – 16%
- Guidance from physician – 14%

Additionally, Humana's survey also assessed why individuals switch their coverage. The reasons:

- Better quality plan – 64%
- Cheaper plan – 54%
- My plan was cancelled – 50%
- Better drug coverage – 47%
- To stay with physician – 45%
- More or better customer service – 38%
- More wellness programs or features – 29%

It should be noted in the two questions asked above respondents could give more than one answer.

Each year there are new Medicare health plans and prescription drug plans which are offered by the private health care insurance companies. If you already work with a licensed insurance agent, early October is a great time to call them and make an appointment to do your Medicare plan review. All new plan information is usually available beginning October 1st each year for the coming year. For 2013 AEP will begin again on October 15th and end December 7th. If you want to change plans you must do it no later than December 7th.

To summarize, these are reasons why you should conduct a review of your current plan each year.

- Change in prescription drugs or dosage levels.
- Prescriptions change formulary tiers.
- Existing Medicare plan becomes no longer available.
- An increase in out-of-pocket costs.
- Access to preferred physicians changes.
- Access to preferred hospitals where medical procedures are done changes.
- Increase in plan premiums.
- Poor customer service.
- Star rating of the plan has been lowered.
- Plan is now considered a low performing plan by CMS.
- Change in beneficiary's health.
- Change in physicians who accept the plan.
- Loss of retiree benefits from a former employer.
- Moved to another county within your state or you've moved to a new state altogether.

Don't be misinformed and do your homework. If you find it too confusing or don't want to invest the time, find someone who is will to help you. You deserve the best quality of care you can find.

"No longer will older Americans be denied the healing miracle of modern medicine. No longer will illness crush and destroy the savings that they have so carefully put away over a lifetime so that they might enjoy dignity in their later years. No longer will young families see their own incomes, and their own hopes, eaten away simply because they are carrying out their deep moral obligations to their parents, and to their uncles, and their aunts."

President's Remarks at the Signing of the Medicare Bill

Lyndon B. Johnson
36th President of the United States
37th Vice President of the United States
Senate Majority Leader
Senate Minority Leader
Senate Majority Whip
Democratic U.S. Senator – Texas

CHAPTER FIVE

ORIGINAL MEDICARE PART A

Many believe that Medicare is completely free and covers everything. Wrong! Original Medicare is composed of two programs: Part A and Part B. What they cover is very specific. There are few restrictions on where you get care and coverage is flexible. The downside is that it can leave significant out-of-pocket costs you are responsible for if you have a major medical event. Individuals who are eligible for Medicare coverage have their Medicare Part A premiums entirely waived, if the following circumstances apply:

- Are 65 years or older and U.S. citizens or have been permanent legal residents for 5 continuous years and they or their spouse have paid Medicare taxes for at least 10 years (40 quarters).

- Are under age 65, disabled and have been receiving either Social Security Disability Insurance (SSDI) benefits or Railroad Retirement Board disability benefits. They must receive one of these benefits for at least **24 months** from date of entitlement (first disability payment) before becoming eligible to enroll in Medicare.
- Are receiving continuing dialysis for End Stage Renal Disease (ENRD) or need a kidney transplant.
- Are eligible for SSDI and have amyotrophic lateral sclerosis (ALS or Lou Gehrig's disease).

Those who do not meet these criteria and are 65 and older must pay a monthly premium to remain enrolled in Medicare Part A. According to the CMS, 99% of Medicare beneficiaries do not pay premiums for Part A. See Chapter 4 for enrollment specifics regarding Part A.

MEDICARE PART A: HOSPITALIZATION INSURANCE

Medicare Part A covers five areas of health care.

- Inpatient Care in Hospitals
- Inpatient Care in a Skilled Nursing Facility
- Nursing Home Care Services
- Hospice Care Services
- Inpatient Care in a Religious Nonmedical Health Care Institution

Hospitalization Coverage

Medicare Part A provides coverage for hospital care. This includes:

- Inpatient hospital care
- Skilled nursing facility care
- Long-term care hospitals

Inpatient Hospital Care

Hospitalization covers inpatient care in hospitals such as critical access hospitals and inpatient rehabilitation facilities. These costs include:

- Semi-private room
- Meals
- General nursing
- Medications as part of your inpatient treatment
- Hospital services and supplies
- All but the first three pints of blood. However, if the hospital gets blood from a blood bank at no charge you shouldn't have to pay for it or replace it.

Medicare does not cover and **excludes:**

- Private duty nursing.
- Private room unless medically necessary.
- Television and telephone in your room (if there's a separate charge for these items.
- Personal care items, such as slippers or razors.

Inpatient mental health care coverage is limited 190 days per lifetime.

Skilled Nursing Facility Care

Part A covers skilled nursing care in a skilled nursing facility (SNF) under certain conditions for a limited time. These Medicare covered services include but are not limited to:

- Semi-private room
- Meals
- Skilled nursing care
- Physical and occupational therapy (Part B)
- Speech language pathology services (Part B)
- Medical social services
- Medications
- Medical supplies and equipment used in the facility
- Ambulance transportation to the nearest supplier of needed services which are not available at the SNF.
- Dietary counseling. A registered dietician or nutritional professional who meets certain requirements can provide these services which can include nutritional assessment, one-on-one counseling and therapy services.

Long-Term Care Hospitals

Long-term care hospitals (LTCH) specialize in treating patients that have more than one serious condition and who may improve with time and care, then return to home. This is not to be confused with long-term care facilities. You will not have to pay a second deductible for your care in a LTCH if:

- You are transferred to a LTCH directly from an acute care hospital.
- You are admitted to a LTCH within 60 days of being discharged from an inpatient hospital stay.

There are deductibles and coinsurance amounts you're responsible for. These deductibles and coinsurance amounts are increasing for 2014. For each benefit period, Medicare pays all covered costs except the Medicare Part A deductible, which for 2014 is $1,216 during the first 60 days and coinsurance amounts for hospital stays that last beyond 60 days but no more than 150 days. For each benefit period you pay:

- A total deductible of $1,216 for a hospital stay lasting from 1-60 days.
- $304 coinsurance per day for days 61-90 of a hospital stay.
- Days 91 and beyond: $608 coinsurance per each "lifetime reserve day" after day 90 for each benefit period in 2014.
- Beyond lifetime reserve days you are responsible for all hospital costs.

Lifetime reserve days are additional days Medicare will pay for when you're in the hospital for more than 90 days. You have a total of 60 reserve days which can be used during your lifetime. For each lifetime reserve Medicare pays all covered costs except for a daily coinsurance.

Staying overnight in a hospital doesn't always mean you're an inpatient. **For Medicare purposes you're considered an inpatient the day a physician formally admits you to a hospital with a physician order.** Many Medicare beneficiaries', who thought they were admitted to a hospital, instead had observation status. This is a Medicare classification which can cost individuals thousands of extra dollars if they need post-hospital nursing care. Most states don't require hospitals to notify patients of their admission status. Medicare covers the first 100 days of care in a skilled nursing facility but only for patients who were first formally admitted to a hospital for three consecutive days.

Federal data shows the number of Medicare patients classified as under observation has jumped sharply in recent years to 1.4 million in 2011 from 920,000 in 2006. This trend is not limited to patients who spend less than 48 hours in the hospital. The number of observation stays, lasting more than 48 hours, totaled 112,000 in 2011 compared with just 27,600 in 2006.

If you're going to be in a hospital overnight always ask the physician if you're going to be an inpatient, outpatient or have observation status. Otherwise you may be the recipient of an extremely large and unwanted hospital bill which you may now need to file an appeal with Medicare, which is another issue. The Center for Medicare Advocacy has a self-help packet which explains the observation status issue in detail and provides detailed guidance for filing appeals at www.medicareadvocacy.org/self-help-packet-for-medicare-observation-status/.

Skilled Nursing Care

For qualified skilled nursing care it must be a Medicare-certified facility. There needs to be a minimum 3-day medically necessary prior inpatient hospitalization stay for a related illness or injury. Transfer to a Medicare-certified facility within 30 days from hospital discharge must occur. The services in the nursing home must be for a condition that was treated during hospitalization (conditions test apply). Your physician must certify that you need daily skilled care like intravenous injections or physical therapy.

Medicare coverage will pay in full the first 20 days. For a skilled nursing facility the coinsurance amount in 2014 is $152.00 per day for days 21 through 100 for each benefit period compared to $148 in 2013. There is no coverage after 100 days. **The deductible for Part A is not an annual deductible but per episode of care deductible.** Part A doesn't cover copays, long-term care or custodial care such as a nursing facility.

Home Health Care

A physician or certain health care providers who work with a physician must see you face-to-face before the physician can certify you need home health services. To qualify the beneficiaries' physician must have determined medical care is needed in the home and the physician has prepared a written plan of care. Needed care must include:

- Intermittent (not full time) skilled nursing care.
- Physical therapy.
- Speech therapy.

- Continued occupational services.

The beneficiary must be home-bound, which means leaving home is a major effort. Absences from home must be infrequent and of short duration to receive medical care. If a Home Health Care Agency is used it must be Medicare approved. Medicare Part A will cover 100% of **medically necessary**, Medicare approved home health care visits. Any Durable Medical Equipment (DME), such as wheelchairs, hospital beds, oxygen and walkers which may be needed Medicare will pay 80% of approved charges leaving you responsible to pay for the remaining 20%. Medicare does NOT cover or pay for:

- 24 hour-a-day care at home.
- Meals delivered to your home
- Homemaker services such as cooking, cleaning or shopping
- Personal care.

Hospice Care

If you qualify for hospice care you'll have a specially trained team and support staff to help you and your family members cope with your illness. The beneficiary must have their physician certify that they're terminally ill and have 6 months or less to live. If you're already getting hospice care a hospice physician or nurse practitioner will need to see you about 6 months after you entered hospice to recertify that you're still terminally ill. Hospice care is usually provided for in your home and includes the following services when your physician includes them in the plan of care for palliative care for your terminal illness. You pay nothing for hospice care but there is a copayment for drugs and a coinsurance charge for inpatient respite care. Hospice coverage includes:

- Physician services.
- Nursing care.
- Medical equipment.
- Medical supplies.
- Medications for symptom control of pain.
- Hospice aid and homemaker services.
- Physical and occupational therapy.
- Speech language pathology services.
- Social work services.
- Dietary counseling.
- Grief and loss counseling for you and your family.
- Short-term inpatient care.
- Short-term respite care.
- Any other Medicare covered services needed to manage your pain and other symptoms related to your terminal illness, as recommended by your hospice team.

Hospice doesn't pay for your stay in a facility (room and board) unless the hospice medical team determines you need short-term inpatient stays for pain and symptom management which can't be addressed at home. Drugs for symptom control and pain relief are subject to a copay of up to $5.00 per prescription.

Medicare also covers inpatient respite care, which is care you get in a Medicare-approved facility so that your usual caregiver can rest. You can stay up to 5 days each time you get respite care. Inpatient respite care is subject to 5% coinsurance payment. You can continue to get hospice care as long as the hospice medical director or hospice physician recertifies that you're terminally ill.

When you make the decision to choose hospice care you have decided you no longer want care to cure your illness and/or you physician has determined efforts to cure your illness are not working. Medicare will not cover any of these once you choose hospice care:

- Treatments intended to cure your illness.
- Prescription drugs to cure your illness.
- Care from any hospice provider that was not set up by the hospice medical team.
- Room and board.
- Care in an emergency room, inpatient facility care or ambulance transportation unless it's either arranged by you hospice team or is unrelated to your terminal illness.

Some additional resources which may help include:

- National Hospice and Palliative Care Organization (NHPCO)
- Hospice Association of America (HAA)
- Hospice Foundation of America (HFA)

Religious Nonmedical Health Care Institution

In these facilities, religious beliefs prohibit conventional and unconventional medical care. If you qualify for hospital or skilled nursing facility care, Medicare will only cover the inpatient, non-religious, non-medical items and services, such as room and board or items and services which don't require a physician's order or prescription.

LATE ENROLLMENT PENALTIES

This was covered in chapter 4 but let's review this point again. If you are not eligible for the premium-free Part A and you don't enroll when you are first eligible, your monthly premium may go up 10%. You'll have to pay this higher premium for twice the number of years you could have had Part A. For example, Jim isn't eligible for premium-free Part A. He first became eligible 2 years ago. Now he wants to enroll in Part A and pay the premium. Jim will have to pay the higher premium for 4 years unless he qualified for an SEP.

PREMIUM COSTS IF YOU HAVE TO PAY FOR PART A COVERAGE

If you aren't eligible for premium-free Part A you can purchase Part A if you meet one of the following conditions:

- You're 65 or older and you have (or are enrolling in) Part B and meet the citizenship and residency requirements.
- You're under 65, disabled and your premium-free Part A coverage ended because you returned to work. If you're under 65 and disabled you can continue to get premium-free Part A for up to 8 1/2 years after you return to work.

There are two different dollar amounts you could be required to pay should you decide to go this route. Both amounts are being reduced for 2014. Beneficiaries who have between 30 and 39 quarters of coverage may buy into Part A at a reduced monthly premium rate of $234 for 2014. This is a $9 reduction from 2013. For those individuals who are not otherwise eligible for premium-free hospital insurance and have less than 30 quarters of Medicare-covered employment will pay a monthly premium of $426 in 2014. This is a $15 reduction from $441 in 2013.

Another option exists for individuals who do not qualify for premium-free Medicare Part A. They may choose to enroll in coverage through the Individual Health Insurance Marketplace rather than purchase the premium Medicare Part A coverage. Individuals who are eligible for premium Medicare Part A are eligible to enroll in a qualified health plan (QHP) through the Marketplace. They may also be eligible for premium tax credits and cost-sharing reductions. To enroll in a QHP in the Marketplace, those individuals must voluntarily end their premium Medicare Part A coverage to avoid duplication of coverage.

A Lawful Permanent Resident (green-card holder) may also be able to purchase premium Medicare Part A coverage without 40 quarters of work if he or she is age 65 or older and has lived in the U.S. continuously for at least five years.

MEDICARE SAVINGS PROGRAMS

The federal government offers Medicare Savings Programs for low-income individuals which the states' administer through Medicaid that pay some or all of beneficiaries' premiums and coinsurance. The programs are called Qualified Medicare Beneficiary (QMB), Specified Low-income Medicare Beneficiary (SLMB), Qualifying Individual (QI) and Qualified Disabled Working Individuals (QDWI). If an individual can answer yes to the following 3 questions, call your State Medicaid Program to see if you qualify for a Medicare Savings Program in your state:

1. Do you have or are you eligible for Medicare Part A?
2. Is your income for 2014 at or below the income limits below?
3. Do you have limited resources below the limits listed below?

Resource limits for the QMB, SLMB, and QI Medicare Savings Programs are $7,080 for one person and $10,620 for a married couple. Resource limits for the QDWI program are $4,000 for one person and $6,000 for a married couple. Countable resources include:

- Money in a checking or savings account
- Stocks
- Bonds

Countable resources **don't** include:

- Your home.
- One car.
- Burial plot.
- Up to $1,500 for burial expenses if you have put that money aside.
- Furniture.
- Other household and personal items.

91

The household income values listed below are for the 48 contiguous states and the District of Columbia. Alaska and Hawaii (not shown) have their own values.

- QMB: $11,736 ($978 monthly) for a single individual and $15,756 ($1,313 monthly) for a married couple. Program helps pay Part A and Part B premiums plus deductibles, copays and coinsurance is guaranteed if you meet the qualifications.
- SLMB: $14,028 ($1,169 monthly) for a single individual and $18,852 ($1,571 monthly) for a married couple. Program helps pay Part B premium and has no fixed budget. Everyone who qualifies gets the benefit.
- QI: $15,756 ($1,313 monthly) for a single individual and $21,180 ($1,765 monthly) for a married couple. Program helps pay Part B premium but program has a fixed budget. When the money is exhausted no one else can qualify that year.
- QDWI: $46,980 ($3,915 monthly) for a single individual and $63,060 ($5,255 monthly) for a married couple. Program helps pay for Part A premiums only.

Information is available at 1-800-MEDICARE (1-800-633-4227), Social Security at 1-800-772-1213. For individuals who have hearing difficulties and/or are speech impaired, information is available at TTY/TDD 1-877-486-2048. Ask for information about Medicare Savings Programs.

CHAPTER SIX

ORIGINAL MEDICARE PART B

Original Medicare Part B is a voluntary program which covers the medical services component of your health care. It was originally designed as a fee-for-service platform. Only Part B charges a monthly premium assuming you are eligible for and have premium-free Part A. Part B helps cover medically-necessary services like physician's services, outpatient care, durable medical equipment, home health services, and other medical services that are needed to diagnose or treat your medical condition and which meet accepted standards of care. Part B also covers some preventive services.

MEDICARE PART B: MEDICAL COVERAGE

Part B covers two types of medical services:

- Medically-necessary services: services or supplies that are needed to diagnose or treat your medical condition and meet accepted standards of medical practice.
- Preventive services: health care to prevent illness (like the flu) or detect it at an early stage, when treatment is most likely to work best.

If you obtain these preventive services from a health care provider who accepts assignment you usually pay nothing.

Medicare may cover some services and tests more often than the timeframes listed if needed to diagnose a condition. Part B premiums increased in 2012 for the first time since 2009. Such increases used to be routine before that. There is a law that prevents premiums from rising if Social Security's cost-of-living adjustment isn't enough to cover the increase. During the low inflation environment which prevailed following the Great Financial Crisis there were no increases because there were no increases in Social Security payments. See Chapter 4 for enrollment specifics regarding Part B.

PREMIUM COSTS

The standard Part B premium for 2014 is $104.90. This is the same as in 2013, which was a $5.00 increase over the 2012 premium of $99.90. The last five years have been among the slowest periods of average Part B premium growth in the programs' history. According to Jonathan Blum, CMS principal deputy administrator, he noted that for the third year in a row Medicare premium costs are meeting or beating expectations. Medicare premiums for 2014 are lower than the $109.10 they were projected to be in 2014.

If you have a high income you may be considered a high earner, in which case you will pay the standard premium plus a fixed dollar amount based on your modified adjusted gross income (MAGI), as reported on **your federal tax return from 2 years earlier**. The Social Security Administration (SSA), which keeps track of income for Medicare premium calculations, will look back two years on your Federal tax returns. It is a two year period because that is the most recent tax return information provided to Social Security by the IRS. For those who become eligible for Medicare in 2014, the SSA will base their premium assessment on your 2012 federal tax return which was filed in 2013.

There are five Medicare income brackets. Currently less than 5% of beneficiaries are affected by these income-related premiums. High income beneficiaries are defined as singles earning more than $85,000 and couples, filing jointly, exceeding $170,000. If you're a high income beneficiary and you are single and filed an individual tax return, or married and filed a joint tax return, your premium is based on your modified adjusted gross income (MAGI). MAGI is the total of your adjusted gross income (gross income minus adjustments to income) plus tax-exempt interest income. If this exceeds $85,000 for single individuals or $170,000 for those married the following premiums will apply for 2014 based on your 2012 Federal Income Tax Return. These income levels are the same as they were in 2013.

- Individuals with a MAGI greater than $85,000 and less than or equal to $107,000 and married couples with a MAGI greater than $170,000 and less than or equal to $214,000. Standard premium + $42.00. **Total Premium $146.90**.
- Individuals with a MAGI greater than $107,000 and less than or equal to $160,000 and married couples with a MAGI greater than $214,000 and less than or equal to $320,000. Standard premium + $104.90. **Total Premium $209.80**.
- Individuals with a MAGI greater than $160,000 and less than or equal to $214,000 and married couples with a MAGI greater than $320,000 and less than or equal to $428,000. Standard premium + $167.80. **Total Premium $272.70**.
- Individuals with a MAGI greater than $214,000 and married couples with a MAGI greater than $428,000. Standard premium + $230.80. **Total Premium $335.70**.

If you are married and lived with your spouse at some time during the taxable year but filed a separate tax return, the following premiums will apply:

- Individuals with a MAGI less than or equal to $85,000. **Standard premium of $104.90**.
- Individuals with a MAGI greater than $85,000 and less than or equal to $129,000. Standard premium + $167.80. **Total Premium $272.70**.
- Individuals with a MAGI greater than $129,000. Standard premium + $230.80. **Total Premium $335.70**.

If you're receiving Social Security, RRB or Civil Service benefits, your Part B premium will be deducted from your benefit payment. If you don't get these benefit payments and choose to sign up for Part B you will receive a bill. If you choose to buy Part A because you don't qualify for premium-free Part A you will always receive a bill for your premium due.

FUTURE PREMIUM PLANNING

This book is not about financial planning, however, one concept is appropriate for discussion here. Traditional retirement planning typically emphasizes investing in tax-deferred investment vehicles such as 401(k)'s and traditional IRA's. In addition, many financial advisors favor the strategy of delaying Social Security benefits until age 70 to optimize the largest cash benefit available to you. Many advisors also advocate delaying distributions from those tax-deferred investment accounts until age 70, when required minimum distributions (RMD) must begin from these accounts. This combination of RMD's from tax-qualified retirement plans, the taxable portion of Social Security benefits and in some cases income from pensions could boost aggregate household income levels quickly which may trigger permanent increases in Medicare premiums which beneficiaries will have to pay. This surge in taxable income at age 70 may not only increase Medicare premiums but you could also see your taxes increase. Go even $1 over the previous discussed thresholds and Medicare will charge you a higher Part B premium. For 2014, the difference between a MAGI of $85,000 and $85,001 for a single individual will result in $504 more in Medicare Part B premiums for the year. Higher income beneficiaries will also pay more for Medicare Part D Prescription Drug premiums which we'll cover in a later chapter.

So how might you keep the potential Medicare premium costs down? Cash value life insurance doesn't trigger higher Medicare premiums as policy distributions and loans do not count in the Medicare MAGI calculation. Tax-free ROTH IRA distributions also are exempt from the Medicare MAGI calculation. Health savings accounts (HSA) are another source of tax-free income in retirement as long as the monies withdrawn are used to pay health care expenses, which can include Medicare premiums. Finally, proceeds from a reverse mortgage and certain distributions from annuities in non-qualified accounts. Individuals in their 50s and early 60s may want to consider these deferred annuities held in a non-qualified account which can act as longevity insurance and minimize taxable income in retirement without the restrictions RMDs. Depending on your tax situation, converting some traditional IRA funds to a Roth IRA account before Medicare eligibility may be another option. Consult your tax expert in these matters.

Finding a financial advisor who specializes in retirement income planning could well be worth your time. Modeling these income flows and understanding their tax implications can help you identify potential "bumps" in the road; giving you time to identify alternative withdrawal strategies to reduce your reportable income. As you get further into retirement and approach that magical age of 70, there are fewer opportunities to optimize those cash-flows.

MEDICAL SERVICES AND ASSIGNMENT

One of the things you will learn as a Medicare recipient is whether or not your health care providers accept assignment. Assignment is an agreement by your physician, other health care provider or supplier who will be paid directly by Medicare, to accept the payment amount Medicare approves for the service, and not to bill you for any more than the Medicare deductible and/or co-insurance. You most likely will pay more for physicians or providers who don't accept assignment.

If the Part B deductible applies you must pay all costs until you meet the yearly Part B deductible before Medicare begins to pay its share. The deductible for Part B in 2014 is $147.00. This is the same as it was for 2013. Then, after your deductible is met you typically pay 20% of the Medicare-approved amount of the service if the physician or other health care provider accepts assignment. **There is no yearly limit or cap for what you pay out-of-pocket.**

COVERED SERVICES

Medicare may cover some services and tests more often than the established timeframes if needed to diagnose a condition. You pay nothing for most preventive services if you get the services from a physician or other health care provider who accepts assignment. For some preventive services you may have to pay a deductible, coinsurance, or both. Listed below are some of the medical services which Medicare covers. Refer to "Your Medicare Coverage" at www.medicare.gov/coverage/preventive-and-screening-services.html for specific details concerning each one of these procedures and how often it is covered. Is there is a test or procedure you don't see listed here, you can easily type it in to see if Medicare covers it or not.

- Abdominal Aortic Aneurysm Screening
- Alcohol Misuse Counseling
- Ambulance Services
- Ambulatory Surgical Centers
- Blood
- Bone Mass Measurement (Bone Density)
- Breast Cancer Screening (Mammograms)
- Cardiac Rehabilitation
- Cardiovascular Disease (Behavioral Therapy)
- Cardiovascular Screenings
- Cervical and Vaginal Cancer Screening
- Chemotherapy
- Chiropractic Services (Limited)
- Clinical Research Studies
- Colorectal Cancer Screenings
- Defibrillator (Implantable Automatic)
- Depression Screening
- Diabetes Screenings
- Diabetes Self-Management Training
- Diabetes Supplies*
- Physician and Other Health Care Provider Services
- Durable Medical Equipment-DME (like walkers)*
- EKG (Electrocardiogram Screening)
- Emergency Department Services
- Eyeglasses (Limited)
- Federally Qualified Health Center Services
- Shots – Flu, Hepatitis B and Pneumococcal

- Foot Exams and Treatment
- Glaucoma Tests
- Hearing and Balance Exams
- Hepatitis B Shots
- HIV Screening
- Home Health Services
- Kidney Dialysis Services and Supplies
- Kidney Disease Education Services
- Laboratory Services
- Medical Nutrition Therapy Services
- Mental Health Care (Outpatient)
- Obesity Screening and Counseling
- Occupational Therapy
- Outpatient Hospital Services
- Outpatient Medical and Surgical Services and Supplies
- Physical Therapy
- Pneumococcal Shot
- Prescription Drugs (Very Limited)
- Prostate Cancer Screenings
- Prosthetic/Orthotic Items*
- Pulmonary Rehabilitation
- Rural Health Clinic Services
- Second Surgical Opinions
- Sexually Transmitted Infections Screening and Counseling
- Speech Language Pathology Services
- Surgical Dressing Services
- Telehealth
- Tests (other than lab tests)
- Tobacco Use Cessation Counseling
- Transplants and Immunosuppressive Drugs
- Travel Outside the United States (very limited for emergency care only)

- Urgently-Needed Care
- "Welcome to Medicare" Preventive Visit
- Yearly "Wellness" Visit

Note * Items – In all areas of the country you must get your covered equipment, supplies, replacement or repair services from a Medicare-approved supplier for Medicare to pay. Some area of the country may have a DME Competitive Bidding Program, which in order to get certain items you must use specific suppliers called "contract suppliers" or Medicare will not pay for the item and you will likely pay full price.

NON-COVERED SERVICES

Medicare does NOT cover the following items or services.

- Most prescriptions
- Long-term care
- Custodial care
- Routine dental or eye care
- Cosmetic surgery
- Acupuncture
- Hearing aids
- Exams for hearing aids
- Routine foot care
- Custodial care is non-skilled personal care. It is designed to help individuals with six activities of daily living like bathing, dressing, eating, toileting, continence and transferring (getting in and out of bed or a chair).

PRESCRIPTION DRUG COVERAGE

For the most part Medicare doesn't cover most prescription drugs. If you're currently not taking many prescription drugs this may not be an issue at the moment. However, if you are taking an extensive list of prescription drugs as you turn 65 you may want to consider alternative health care coverage.

Most Medicare Advantage Part C plans will include prescription drug coverage. Your other choice will be a standalone Medicare Prescription Part D Drug plan. Both will be covered extensively in subsequent chapters.

WELCOME TO MEDICARE PREVENTIVE VISIT

Once you are enrolled in Part B, anytime during the first 12 months you can call your physician and let them know you would like to schedule your "Welcome to Medicare" preventive visit. You pay nothing if your health care provider accepts assignment.

During this visit you will get a review of your medical and social history related to your health and education. There is counseling about preventive services which are available as well as preventive screenings for abdominal aortic aneurysm and electrocardiogram (EKG), shots and referrals for other care which if needed.

For more comprehensive details on the covered services listed above and the frequency of coverage see the Medicare publication, *Medicare & You – 2014*, beginning with page 33 or online at www. medicare.gov/. Click the Help & Resources tab on the right.

"I think that age as a number is not nearly as important as health. You can be in poor health and be pretty miserable at 40 or 50. If you're in good health, you can enjoy things into your 80s."

Bob Barker – Age 90
Former Television Game Show Host
The Price is Right – 1972-2007
Truth or Consequences – 1956-1975

CHAPTER SEVEN

MEDICARE ADVANTAGE PART C PLANS

The *Balanced Budget Act (BBA) of 1997*, enacted August 5, 1997, was an omnibus legislative package using the budget reconciliation process and was designed to balance the federal budget by 2002. With the passage of the BBA, Medicare beneficiaries were given the option to receive their Medicare benefits through private health insurance plans instead of through the original Medicare system. These programs were originally known as Medicare+Choice or Part C plans and were offered by private health insurance companies. Pursuant to the *Medicare Prescription Drug, Improvement, and Modernization Act of 2003*, the compensation and business practices changed for insurers that offer these plans and Medicare+Choice plans became known as Medicare Advantage plans. See Chapter 4 for enrollment specifics regarding these plans.

MEDICARE ADVANTAGE PART C

Medicare Advantage plans are offered by private insurance companies approved by and contracted with Medicare. With Medicare Advantage the insurance company pays all claims submitted by health care providers instead of Medicare. Medicare pays a monthly fee to the insurance company for each enrollee. These insurance companies must follow rules set by Medicare and plans are filed on an annual basis with Medicare. These plans are also referred to as Part C or MA plans also. According to a report from the Kaiser Family Foundation, 28% of the Medicare population, over 14 million beneficiaries are now enrolled in a Medicare Advantage plan. Total enrollment has grown by 30%, 3.3 million individuals, since 2010.

Examples of MA plans include HMOs, PPOs and PFFS plans. The member does not lose their Medicare Part A and Part B coverage and they need to continue to pay their Part B premium each month. Medicare Part C plans combine hospital and outpatient medical services into one package for plan members covering both Part A and Part B. These plans usually include prescription drug coverage also. Medicare Advantage plans may also offer additional benefits and services beyond what you get by having just original Medicare coverage. In addition, most plans are state and/or county specific. Which state or specific county you live can affect the costs you pay and benefits received.

These plans can and do change each year. Each MA plan can charge different out-of-pocket costs and have different rules for how you get services, like whether you need a referral to see a specialist or if you have to

106

go to only doctors, facilities or suppliers that belong to the plan for non-emergency or non-urgent care. Cuts in subsidies to the insurance providers are scheduled so this may affect the level of benefits offered in the future. Not all Medicare Advantage plans work the same way. Before you join, discuss the plan's rules, what the costs will be and whether the plan will meet your health care needs.

TYPES OF MEDICARE ADVANTAGE PLANS

There are different types of MA plans which are offered by private health insurance companies. These plans may vary in terms of costs and benefits offered from one health insurance provider to another. Not all Medicare Advantage plans work the same way so before you join take the time to find and compare the Medicare Advantage health plans in your area. Not all plans which may be available in the state may be available in your service area.

Health Maintenance Organization (HMO, HMO-POS)

An HMO plan must cover all Medicare Part A and Part B health care services. Some HMOs also cover additional benefits, like additional days in the hospital. In most HMOs you can only go to physicians, specialists or hospitals on the plan's list of contracted in-network providers. The one exception is in the case of emergency care. The member must choose a primary care physician (PCP) and referrals may be required for specialist visits. Some services may require pre-authorization.

In the case of a Point-of-Service (POS) plan the member may obtain certain services out-of-network at a higher cost. Your initial costs may be lower than in the original Medicare program. These plans may or may not include prescription drug coverage.

Preferred Provider Organization (PPO)

With this type of plan you use physicians, hospitals and providers that belong to your designated PPO contracted network for the lowest out-of-pocket expenses. Usually these networks are geographically regional or local for the health care providers who are included. You don't have to have a PCP designated and there is no requirement for referrals. You may use physicians, hospitals and providers outside of the network but there will be an additional cost. This plan may or may not include prescription drug coverage.

Special Needs Plan (SNP)

These plans generally limit membership to people with specific diseases or conditions. They tailor their benefits, choose their providers and create their list of covered drugs to best meet the specific needs of the groups they serve. Since they offer all health care services through a single plan, Medicare SNPs can help you manage your different services and health care providers. This is usually a network based plan with a required PCP to be designated. There are usually three types.

- Chronic Condition (C-SNP): You have one or more of the following severe or disabling chronic conditions such as chronic alcohol and other drug dependence, autoimmune disorders, cancer, cardiovascular disorders, chronic heart failure, dementia, diabetes, end-stage liver disease, end-stage renal disease, severe hematologic disorders, HIV/AIDS, chronic lung disorders, chronic and disabling mental health conditions, neurological disorders and stroke.

- Institutional (I-SNP): You live in a nursing home or you require nursing care at home where a long-term care setting is required.
- Dual-Eligible (D-SNP): You have both Medicare and Medicaid which coordinate costs and services.

Each Medicare SNP limits its membership to individuals in one these above groups. All Medicare SNPs include prescription drug coverage.

Private Fee-for-Service (PFFS)

In this type of plan you can go to any Medicare-approved physician or hospital that accepts the plans' terms and conditions of payment. The insurance plan, rather than the Medicare program, decides how much it will pay and what you pay for the services. You may pay more or less for Medicare-covered benefits. You may also have more benefits than with original Medicare Part A and Part B.

Medicare Medical Savings Account (MSA)

A MSA plan combines a high deductible health plan with a bank account. Medicare gives the plan an amount each year for the member's care and the plan deposits a portion of this money into the bank account. You can use the money to pay for health care services during the year. For more information about MSAs visit http://go.usa.gov/irD, to view the booklet, *Your Guide to Medicare Medical Savings Account Plans.*

PREMIUM COSTS

If you enroll in a Medicare Advantage plan you will still need to continue paying your monthly Part B premium. This payment is usually deducted directly from your Social Security or Railroad Retirement Board (RRB) benefits each month if you're receiving those benefits. If you're not enrolled in Social Security or RRB you will need to set up payment by either an Electronic Funds Transfer (ETF) with your bank or by a Coupon Book.

Premiums for the plans themselves can range from a low dollar premium to $0 each month. For 2014, the $0 dollar premium plan is becoming more prevalent. **Some plans may even reimburse you back some or all of your Part B premiums each month.** Costs and benefits provided may be different depending on which type of Medicare Advantage plan you enroll in. Beware if you hear the word "free" used when someone describes the cost of the plan! Remember that premiums are different from copays and coinsurance, which are usually a component of each plan. Copayments are usually a set dollar amount while coinsurance payments are a percentage of the charges incurred for services rendered. These costs are described in the *Summary of Benefits* section within the plan document for each type of plan. The *Summary* *of Benefits* will compare coverage and costs of original Medicare with those of the specific plan document, such as an HMO, HMO-POS, HMO-SNP or PPO plan. The insurance company offering the plan determines how much it pays and how much the member pays for each Medicare covered service.

Copayments and coinsurance may be higher than those in original Medicare. One big advantage of MA plans is the member's costs are usually capped each year for covered services. This maximum annual out-of-pocket expense doesn't exist with original Medicare. There is no limit to what you could be responsible for if you have a major medical event. So with a MA plan the member knows exactly what their worst case scenario could be in terms of costs. This could still be a significant amount of money for someone in their later years if they max out their out-of-pocket expenses due to unforeseen health issues and are on a fixed income budget each month.

Later in this chapter I'll provide more specific information for those readers who live in Florida. I'm sure this material presented will be similar to how plan documents are structured in other states though costs and additional benefits provided could be significantly different from state to state.

COVERED MEMBER BENEFITS

Medicare Advantage plans must cover all of the services that original Medicare covers in Part A and Part B except hospice care. Original Medicare covers hospice care even if you're in a Medicare Advantage plan. In addition most plans offer prescription drug coverage. Unlike original Medicare that lets you see what ever physician you want, most Medicare Advantage plans have a provider network the member must use. These provider networks are usually regional so if you spend part of the year somewhere else and you need care it may be considered out of network and may or may not be covered.

ADDITIONAL MEMBER BENEFITS

In addition to the covered medical and hospitalization benefits which are combined in Medicare Advantage, most plans will also have additional member benefits included in their plans at $0 or low cost to you. These benefits may include fitness memberships, preventive dental care, routine vision care including eyeglasses, and hearing care including hearing aids.

Some plans may also offer telephone access to registered nursing professionals who can help with general questions related to health care and nutrition. They usually cannot diagnose problems or recommend specific treatments and are NOT a substitute for your physician's care.

Generally, health care must be obtained and received in the service area of your plan. This may be county specific or state wide depending on the type of plan and insurance company. Additional travel coverage may also be included in the plan which is generally confined to domestic travel only, NOT out of the country. Some insurance companies offer coverage outside of your plan area, such as when traveling out of your residential state. This additional coverage may include an entire state or just specific counties within that state and not all states may be included in the coverage area. If you travel the USA frequently seeing the grandkids or just vacationing, be sure to check with customer service of the plan for these additional travel benefits, what actions need to be taken on your part to activate the benefits and if any restrictions are involved. Generally many plans require the insurance company to be notified if your travel plans are for an extended period of time in order to activate your travel benefits.

The exception to out of the country medical coverage is if you need emergency care. All plans provide coverage for emergency care worldwide. Emergency care should not be confused with urgently needed care which is usually not covered if you're traveling out of the country. If you travel out of the country frequently you'll want to read the chapter on Medicare Supplement plans. There can be more generous travel coverage with some of those plans than with an MA.

These additional member benefits can be quite good so be sure to take advantage of them. They can add up to some great cost savings.

SWITCHING PLANS

There is a misunderstanding among many individuals that if you have a pre-existing health condition and you are already enrolled in a Medicare Advantage plan you can't switch plans. This is not true. The Medicare Advantage plan must accept you irrespective of any pre-existing health conditions. The only exception to this is if you have been diagnosed with or have End Stage Renal Disease (ESRD). If you are diagnosed with ESRD while on a Medicare Advantage plan the plan is required to maintain your acceptance in the plan. The condition may prevent you from changing plans in the future though.

During the Medicare Annual Enrollment Period, which for 2013 runs from October 15 through December 7, you have the ability to switch between the various Medicare Advantage plans offered by the insurance companies. If you switch, new plan benefits for coverage will become effective January 1, 2014. For instances:

- You can change from original Medicare to a Medicare Advantage (MA) plan.
- You can change from an MA plan back to original Medicare.
- You can switch from a MA plan to a different MA plan from another insurance company.
- You can switch from a MA plan that doesn't offer prescription drug coverage to a MA plan that does.
- You can switch from a MA plan that offers prescription drug coverage to one that doesn't.

Medicare Advantage plans do change each year. New plans are introduced and some may be dropped. Each fall you will receive your ANOC (Annual Notice of Change) letter from your Medicare Advantage provider, usually by September 30th. This letter outlines any changes which will occur for your plan in the upcoming year. This is the best time to do a Medicare Plan review. Has your health changed in the past year? Has your income levels changed? Are you taking any new drugs? You may find you're able to enroll in a better plan which will cost you less money.

Who doesn't want to save some money? You'll never know if you don't investigate what's new.

If upon investigation of various plans you decide that switching plans makes sense. Before you switch, make sure all the physicians you go to, hospitals used for procedures and prescription drugs taken will be covered by the new plan. **Make NO assumptions about plan benefits and coverage when you decide to switch plans. Double check everything! It could save you a lot of aggravation later.**

LIVING IN FLORIDA

This section is designed for readers of the book who live in the state of Florida. As a licensed insurance agent in Florida I am appointed with a number of health insurance companies which offer Medicare Advantage plans. While space doesn't permit me to go into all the specifics of each type of plan offered by those insurance companies, I can provide some generalizations about Medicare Advantage plans in Florida. What follows is NOT a solicitation for the purchase of a Medicare Advantage plan but is meant for general and educational information only. *This may or may not be representative of the costs you see and benefits offered in states other than Florida.* The plan information is for 2013, for plans effective January 1, 2014.

In Florida, what county you live in will determine which insurance companies and which type of Medicare Advantage plans are offered. Insurance companies do not always offer their plan types in every single county. For example, each insurance company can have multiple designs of their HMO plan throughout the state. Costs and benefits covered may be different in Hillsborough County vs. Miami-Dade County. Up in the Jacksonville area they might offer an HMO but no HMO-POS or SNP plans. Some insurance companies will offer plans based on regional areas such as South Florida, Central Florida, West Central Florida and so forth. The same plan is offered within a cluster of counties. Also, some insurance companies will choose be far more competitive in certain areas of the state and not so in others.

Medicare Advantage Plan Document

If this is the first time you're being exposed to all this it can feel like quite a daunting experience. All the information you need to digest, comprehend and then formulate a decision on which plan type and which insurance company will provide you the best health care coverage in the coming year can be overwhelming. We're going to provide a brief synopsis of what a Medicare Advantage plan document will have in it. These plan documents are sometimes also referred to as the Enrollment Kit. We'll cover specific parts of a plan document throughout the remainder of this section and in those for Part D Prescription Drug and Medicare Supplement/Medigap plans. What may be included within the plan document package is:

- Benefits at a Glance.
- CMS Star Rating.
- Preventive Care Coverage
- Summary of Benefits.
- Formulary Drug and Tier Levels for the Plan.
- Other Plan Benefits.

116

- Enrollment Process.
- Plan Application Forms.
- Scope of Appointment (SOA) Form.
- Outbound Enrollment and Verification (OEV).

In addition, if an insurance company offers a limited number of plans, such as either an HMO or PPO within a plan area you may see both plans combined within the same plan document. The *Summary of Benefits* section is usually included within the plan document. In some cases it may be a separate *Summary of Benefits* insert as part of the package. Every package from each of the insurance companies, containing all the plan materials will probably be a little different when you open them up.

Monthly Plan Premiums

Most insurance companies are now offering a HMO, HMO-POS and/or PPO plans with a $0 monthly premium for 2104, while a few plans charge a monthly premium. For those plans which charge a monthly premium, the premiums are usually between $35 and $105 each month. You still need to continue paying your Medicare Part B premium either way though. A few plans exist which reimburse the member back some, if not all, of their Medicare Part B premium, which is usually automatically deducted from either their Social Security or RRB benefits each month. They receive this reimbursement as a check from the insurance company. *It may take up to 3 months before you receive your first reimbursement of Medicare Part B premiums.*

117

With SNPs there are many plans with a $0 premium each month also. For those that do charge a premium it is usually less than $25 each month. Some of these plans require that you are receiving assistance from the state of Florida for you to be eligible to enroll.

Covered Benefits

Not all plans are always an apple to apple comparison. This is where understanding your current health situation, what medical services you might need in the coming year and how often you need those medical services is important. Just because a plan has a $0 premium each month doesn't necessarily make it the best plan. If your current health status necessitates you are a heavy user of medical and hospitalization services you could end up paying more when your copays and coinsurance costs are factored in compared to a plan which may have a small monthly premium.

Your best plan is to carve out some time and do a little math to see where your health care costs are coming from. This information will give you your best ability to compare plans to determine which may be most cost effective while providing you optimal coverage and benefits.

Most individuals already understand this concept but we'll quickly review the differences between in-network and out-of-network charges. There can be substantial money differences involved between the two if you're having a lot of office visits or procedures being done. The insurance company determines the in-network participation providers. If any plan has HMO on the cover you must use the in-network providers to have the plan cover expenses, except in an emergency.

You may also need a referral from your PCP for specialist's visits and other diagnostic procedural work. Otherwise you may end up personally responsible for the entire medical bill. A plan with PPO on the cover allows you to see any health care provider though you will pay less if you use the plans' in-network list of health care providers. Also you usually will not need a referral from your PCP for specialist's visits.

For most types of plans your primary care physician (PCP) in-network office visits could have copays between $0 and $40 per visit. Out-of-network PCP visits could have copays between $25 and $50. For a specialist office visits copays could be between $40 and $50 for in-network visits and between $50 and $70 or a 30% to 40% coinsurance payment for an out-of-network visit.

Preventive care and health screening services will usually have $0 copays for in-network service while out-of-network service could have between a 30%-40% coinsurance payment.

For inpatient hospitalization, in-network hospital copays could be between $95 and $395 per day for hospital stays between 1-7 days. Many plans then have a $0 copays thereafter. For out-of-network, inpatient hospital copays could have coinsurance of between 30%-40% from day one. Most plans though don't provide for out-of-network hospital coverage.

For skilled nursing facility (SNF) care in-network copays are based on the number of days SNF care is needed. There are usually 3 tiers for days in most plans. In tier 1, copays can range from $0 to $50 each day. For tier 2, copays can range from $50 to $150 each day and for tier 3, copays range from $0 to $100 each day up until 100 days of care is received. For out-of-network SNF care, out to 49 days there is a copay of $195 per day. From days 50-100 the copay is $0. Other plans can have a flat coinsurance change of 30% per stay.

For outpatient surgery and hospital services copays are between $175 and $275 for in-network care. For out-of-network, outpatient surgery and hospital service usually have 30% coinsurance.

As you can see some of these copays can vary considerable form one insurance company to the next. If you don't need to see a physician on a regular basis this may not be an issue for you. However, if you are experiencing poor health or needing to see a physician several times during the year these copays can add up relatively quickly. In the end you should spend a little time conversing with your spouse or significant other in arriving at a decision. It's a decision you or both of you will have to live with for the next twelve months.

SOME FINAL THOUGHTS ON MEDICARE ADVANTAGE PLANS

There are several items you should be aware of with a Medicare Advantage plan.

- You can only join a plan at certain times during the year. In most cases you're enrolled in a plan for a year.
- As with original Medicare you still have Medicare rights and protections, including the right to appeal a claim denial.

- Check with the plan before you get a service to find out whether they will cover the service and what your costs may be.
- You must follow plan rules, like getting a referral to see a specialist or getting prior approval for certain procedures to avoid higher costs. Check with the plan.
- You can join a MA plan even if you have a pre-existing condition, except for End-Stage Renal Disease.
- If you go to a physician, facility or supplier that doesn't belong to the plan your services may not be covered or your costs could be higher, depending on the type of MA plan you're enrolled in.
- If the plan decides to stop participating in Medicare, you'll have to join another Medicare health plan or return to original Medicare.

As you navigate this process do not underestimate the value of high quality customer service. You may find that the plans offered by the insurance companies in the area in which you live in are similar in scope and design. You won't understand the value of customer service until you have to reach out to them with questions. Ask your friends who may be enrolled in a Medicare Advantage plan what they think of the insurance company they have their plan with.

One last point to emphasize, make sure you read or re-read the plan document and pay particular attention to the *Summary of Benefits* section. This is where the details of the benefits covered by the plan are and what you will pay. Ask questions if you don't understand everything completely.

"Sometimes in this whole Medicare prescription drug debate, we focus on the prescription drug benefit, and I am glad we do because it is the first time we have ever offered real help to seniors, especially the poor, those in need."

John Shimkus
Republican U.S. House of Representatives - Illinois's 15th Congressional District

CHAPTER EIGHT

MEDICARE PRESCRIPTION DRUG PART D PLANS

According to the Centers for Disease Control and Prevention (CDC), 2.6 billion prescriptions were ordered or provided in the U.S. in 2010. Those orders were placed from a list of 35,574 human prescription drugs which are available according to the National Drug Code Directory. Medicare offers voluntary prescription drug coverage to everyone with Medicare. To obtain the prescription drug coverage you must join a plan administered by either a health insurance company or other private company approved by and contracted with Medicare. Each plan can vary in cost and specific drugs covered. Even if you don't take many prescription medications now, it's important for you to consider joining a Medicare Prescription Drug Part D plan if you do not have other creditable drug coverage such as through an employer-sponsored health plan. If you decide **not to join** a Medicare Prescription Drug Part D plan when you're first eligible and you don't have other creditable prescription drug coverage you will likely pay a late enrollment penalty.

If you're enrolled in a Medicare Advantage plan, which includes prescription drug coverage and you join a stand-alone Medicare Prescription Drug Part D plan you'll be disenrolled from your Medicare Advantage plan and returned to original Medicare. There are two ways to get Medicare prescription drug coverage:

1.   Medicare Advantage Plans (MA-PD)

These plans add prescription drug coverage to the Medicare Advantage plan. To join an MA-PD, individuals must be enrolled in both Medicare Part A **and** Part B. In both instances the individual must also live in the service area of the Medicare Advantage plan they wish to enroll in. There's no additional cost for drug coverage other than copays and each type of Medicare Advantage plan will have its own specific formulary. So if you plan to get your drug coverage through a Medicare Advantage plan make sure your prescription drugs are listed in the plan document's formulary listing section and compare the different drug tiers to see which tiers your medications are in.

2.   Medicare Prescription Drug Plan (PDP)

These plans add prescription drug coverage to beneficiaries with original Medicare, some Medicare Cost Plans, Medicare Private Fee-for-Service (PFFS) plans and Medicare Supplement/Medigap plans. In addition you must be entitled to Medicare Part A **and/or** enrolled in Medicare B.

For individuals navigating the Medicare enrollment process for the first time many find understanding the prescription drug program to be the most confusing. **You need to pay attention to the details in what each drug plan offers, drugs covered, which tiers they are in and where your prescriptions can be bought.** Like Medicare Advantage plans, PDPs can change their plans every year with new plans coming out. See Chapter 4 for enrollment and late penalty specifics regarding Medicare Prescription Drug Part D plans.

STANDARD BENEFITS

Eligible Medicare Prescription Drug Part D plans can have an annual deductible, a copayment/coinsurance up to an initial coverage limit, a coverage gap and catastrophic coverage for the rest of the year after an individual incurs out-of-pocket expenses above the annual out-of-pocket threshold. The standard benefit levels are adjusted annually, including all the expenses just previously mentioned.

The yearly deductible is the amount you must pay before your drug plan begins to pay its share of your covered drugs. Some drug plans don't have a deductible. The deductible for these programs can run from $0 to no more than $310 in 2014. This is down from the $325 deductible in 2013. The copayments and coinsurance are amounts you pay for your covered prescriptions after the deductible has been met. These are amounts you pay for your share and your drug plan pays its share for covered drugs. Your actual drug plan costs will vary depending on:

- The plan you choose.
- The drugs you use.
- Whether you go to a pharmacy in your plan's network.
- Whether your drugs are on your plan's formulary.
- Which tier the drugs are in.
- Whether you get "Extra Help" paying your Part D costs.

Is your local pharmacy on the preferred list? Is there a limit to the number of prescription you can get? Do you have to try less expensive alternatives before paying for your current prescription? These are questions you want answers to before you enroll.

DRUG COVERAGE RULES

Medicare drug plans may have the following rules regarding drug coverage:

- *Prior authorization:* You and/or your prescriber must contact the drug plan before you can fill certain prescriptions. Your prescriber may need to show that the drug is medically necessary for the plan to cover it.
- *Quantity limits:* Limits on how much medication you can get at a time. These are set by private insurance companies and/or regulations set by the government. These limits may be in place to ensure safe and efficient use of the medication.

- *Step therapy:* There are effective, clinically proven, lower-cost alternatives to some medications that treat the same health condition. You must try one or more similar, lower cost drugs before the plan will cover the prescribed drug. If the individual has already tried other medications or a provider thinks other drugs are not right for the situation, the individual or his/her physician can ask the plan to cover these medications.

If you or your prescriber believe that one of these coverage rules should be waived, you can ask for an exception. Except for vaccines covered under Medicare Part B, Medicare drug plans must cover all commercially-available vaccines, such as the shingles vaccine when medically necessary to prevent illness.

PREMIUM COSTS

Most prescription drug plans (PDP) charge a monthly premium that varies by plan. You pay this premium in addition to the Medicare Part B premium. The average premium for a drug plan is $32/month. For 2014, not all plans have a deductible but you will pay a higher premium for these plans. Individuals have four options on how to pay for their Part D plan:

- Auto deduction from Social Security. This is usually the most preferred method.
- Auto pay from their bank.
- Auto deduction from a credit card.
- Direct monthly billing.

Contact the drug plan provider you chose if you want your premium deducted from your monthly Social Security payment. Don't call Social Security. Your first deduction will usually take three months to start and three months of premiums will likely be deducted at once. After that only one premium will be deducted each month. You may also see a delay in premiums being withheld if you switch plans. If you want to stop premium deductions and get billed directly contact your drug plan. There are also five income levels for Medicare Part D. Table 8.1 below illustrates the additional premium high earners will need to pay based on their income levels for tax year 2012.

Table 8.1 Additional Premiums for High Income Earners

	If your yearly income in 2012 was		You pay in 2014
File individual tax return	File married & separate tax returns	File married joint tax returns	
$85,000 or less	$85,000 or less	$170,000 or less	Your plan premium
Above $85,000 up to $107,000	Not applicable	Above $170,000 up to $214,00	$12.10 + your plan premium
Above $107,000 up to $160,000	Not applicable	Above $214,000 up to $320,000	$31.10 + your plan premium
Above $ 160,000 up to $214,000	Above $85,000 up to $129,000	Above $320,000 up to $$428,000	$50.20 + your plan premium
Above $214,000	Above $129,000	Above $428,000	$69.30 + your plan premium

Courtesy: Centers for Medicare and Medicaid Services; Medicare – Costs At a Glance

High income earners can expect to pay from just over $12 to slightly more than $69 more each month based on their income plus the plan's monthly premium. This is slightly more than the levels in 2013.

TOTAL DRUG COSTS

The deductible, copayments, coinsurance and coverage gap costs all count towards your total drug costs.

TrOOP

True out-of-pocket (TrOOP) expenses are costs used to move the individual through the coverage gap phase and into the catastrophic phase. These costs can be incurred by the individual or another person on behalf of the individual. TrOOP expenses include:

- Deductible.
- Copayments paid up to the coverage gap.
- While in coverage gap individuals pay 72% of generic drugs and 47.5% of brand name drugs.
- While in the catastrophic phase the individual pays 5% coinsurance or a fixed dollar amount, whichever amount is greater.

The Donut Hole

Medicare drug plans have a coverage gap. This is also known as the donut hole. This means there is a temporary limit on what the drug plan will cover for drugs. The coverage gap begins after you and your drug plan have spent a certain amount for covered drugs. According to CMS, nearly 2.8 million individuals reached the donut hole in the first nine months of 2013. This is an increase of nearly 22% over 2012. Those who have reached the prescription drug coverage gap have saved $2.3 billion. For 2012, seniors saved $2.5 billion and in 2011 saved $2.3 billion on prescriptions.

Figure 8.1 below illustrates a standard Medicare Part D Prescription Drug plan and what you'll pay in 2014, depending on the amount of money you end up spending for prescription drugs.

Figure 8.1 Donut Hole Dilemma

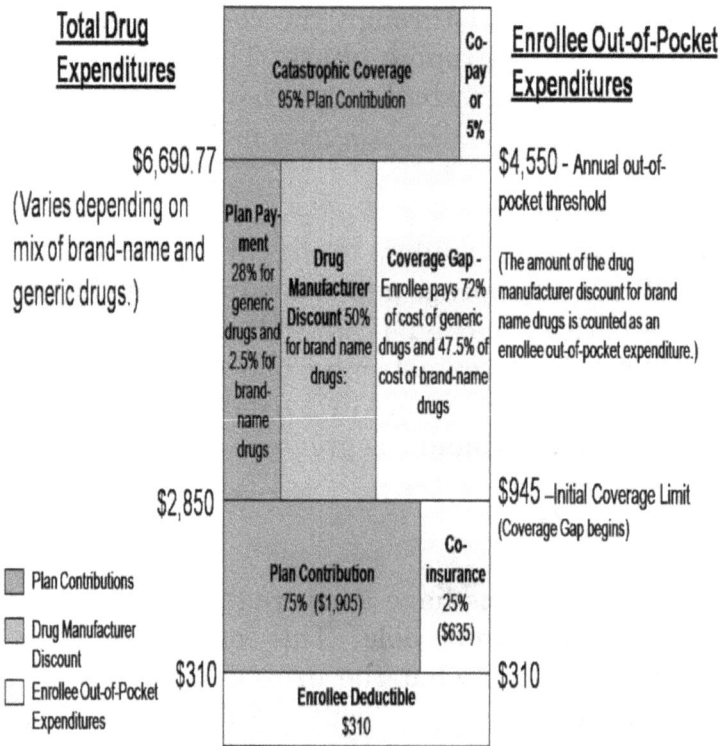

Courtesy: AHIP 2013

As you can see you're responsible for the first $310 of prescriptions before coverage begins. During the initial coverage phase you'll pay a copay which is a flat dollar fee or coinsurance which is a percentage of the drug's total cost for each prescription medication you fill depending on the plan. The PDP pays the rest until your total drug costs (paid by you and the plan) reach the initial coverage limit of $2,850. Then you hit what is called the "donut hole" or coverage gap. This coverage gap in when Medicare beneficiaries have to pay a greater portion of their drug costs. Once you enter the coverage gap you pay 47.5% of the total cost for brand name drugs and 72% of the total cost for generic drugs in 2014. For 2013, the cost for generics was 79% while brand names were the same. The initial coverage limit is also $120 less than it was for 2013, which means more individuals could end up in the coverage gap sooner in 2014. Most PDPs provide no additional coverage while in the coverage gap.

Not everyone will enter the coverage gap though. The following items all count toward you getting out of the coverage gap; your yearly deductible, coinsurance, copayments, the discount you get on brand-name drugs in the coverage gap and what you pay in the coverage gap. The drug plan premium and what you pay for drugs that aren't covered don't count toward getting you out of the coverage gap.

If your out-of-pocket costs reach $4,550 in 2014, you move out of the coverage gap and into catastrophic coverage. In this phase you pay either a copay of $2.25 for generic drugs or $6.35 for brand name drugs or a 5% coinsurance amount to fill prescriptions, whichever is greater. The PDP and Medicare pay the rest until the end of the calendar year.

Since the ACA was enacted in 2010, which included a provision to close the prescription coverage gap, more than 7.1 million seniors and individuals with disabilities that reach the coverage gap have saved $8.3 billion in their prescription drug costs. There are more savings in the coverage gap coming over the next several years. The percentages saved on brand-names and generics while in the coverage gap will increase each year through 2020. In 2020, the savings will then be fixed at 25% for both. Table 8.2 below illustrates when these changes will take place and the lower percentages you'll pay for prescription drugs.

Table 8.2 Future Changes in Drug Coverage

	You will pay this percentage for Brand Name drugs in the Coverage Gap	You will pay this percentage for Generic drugs in the Coverage Gap
2012	50%	86%
2013	47.5%	79%
2014	47.5%	72%
2015	45%	65%
2016	45%	58%
2017	40%	51%
2018	35%	44%
2019	30%	37%
2020	25% thereafter	25% thereafter

Courtesy: Medicare Prescription Drug Coverage, January 2012

EXAMPLE

An example may help to alleviate some of the confusion surrounding this. Ms. Jones has a standard

Medicare Prescription Drug Part D plan. Her deductible is **$310** for 2014. She will pay the first $310 of her drug costs before her plan starts to pay its share. Once she has satisfied the deductible, Ms. Jones pays a copayment and her plan pays its share for each covered drug prescription filled until **their combined amount (plus the deductible) reaches $2,850 in 2014**. From the earlier chart in Figure 8.2, **$310** + **$2,540** (Plan Contribution of 75%; **$1,905** + Coinsurance of 25%; $635 = $2,540) equals **$2,850**. Once Ms. Jones and her plan have spent $2,850 for covered drugs she is in the coverage gap. For 2014, she gets a 47.5% discount on covered brand-name prescription drugs and she pays 72% of the plan's cost for covered generic drugs. What she pays and the amount paid by the drug company counts as out-of-pocket spending and helps her to get out of the coverage gap. Once Ms. Jones spends a **true $4,550 out-of-pocket (TrOOP)** for drug expenses during the year her coverage gap ends. Now she only pays either a small copayment or 5% coinsurance amount for each drug prescription filled, whichever is greater until the end of the calendar year when everything starts over.

FORMULARIES AND TIERS

A formulary is a list of medications covered within the benefit plan. This often represents the level of cost-sharing associated with different groupings of medications. These groupings are usually preferred generics, non-preferred generics, preferred brands and non-preferred brands. A preferred brand name prescription medication is a drug which has been determined by the plan to be as effective as other medications. Some online formularies list only the preferred generic and brand drugs. This is called the Preferred Drug List (PDL). Each PDP develops its formulary through a rigorous clinical evaluation process, including physicians and pharmacists. The CMS provides strict guidelines to the plans regarding types of medications that must be covered. CMS also reviews and approves each plan's formulary.

There are five pharmacy tiers in most prescription drug plans. They also have copays and coinsurance expenses depending on the tier in question. These are:

- Tier 1: Preferred Generic; lowest copayment.
- Tier 2: Non-Preferred Generic; low copayment.
- Tier 3: Preferred Brand; medium copayment.
- Tier 4: Non-Preferred Brand; higher copayment.
- Tier 5: Specialty; coinsurance.

Each PDP will usually have a preferred pharmacy network and other pharmacy network. Copays and coinsurance will be lowest in the preferred network as opposed to going out of the preferred network.

MANAGING PRESCRIPTION DRUG COSTS

There will be more than 200 new Medicare Prescription Drug Part D plans being offered for 2014. Nearly 50 existing plans are leaving the market. Individuals in plans which will not be available in 2014 have a valuable opportunity to study their options during the current AEP. Part D plan cost can change over time. This includes the cost of the premiums, deductibles, copays and coinsurance.

A recent study from the University of Pittsburgh found that 95% of Medicare beneficiaries do not choose the most cost-effective plan. In an analysis done by the Kaiser Family Foundation, for the vast majority of individuals enrolled in a Medicare Part D PDP during the four year period between 2006 and 2010, on average, 87% remained in the same Part D plan even though the plans could change premiums, deductibles, cost-sharing amounts and the list of covered drugs each year. If you've had the same Part D plan for the last 3-4 years now may be the time to compare options. Taking the following steps may lead you to making more cost-effective PDP coverage decisions.

- Review your prescription drug list with your physician. There may be a less expensive brand-name or generic equivalent which will work just as well as what you're currently taking.
- Compare drug plan formularies, coverage tiers and restrictions. What you pay out-of-pocket is largely determined by how well a given plan covers the specific drugs you take. Medicare requires drug plans to cover drugs in every therapeutic class but NOT every drug in a class. One of the drugs you're taking could be in Tier 4 in your plan, for example, and Tier 3 in another plan. Use the 60- or 90-day mail-order pharmacy for your supply of maintenance drugs.
- Evaluate the plan's preferred pharmacies. If you're not filing your prescriptions at one of the plan's preferred pharmacies you could be paying significantly more for your prescriptions.
- Considering a plan with gap coverage? Do the math. Having a plan like that may seem to offer

valuable added protection but you need to determine whether those benefits will offset a much higher premium. For 2013, about 50% of the Part D plans, which offered gap coverage, limited their benefit to generic drugs only. None of the plans provided gap coverage for all drugs on their formulary.

Medicare beneficiaries may not realize they might be able to save hundreds if not thousands of dollars over the year by switching to a PDP which is a better fit.

SWITCHING PLANS

During the Medicare AEP, which for 2013 runs from October 15th through December 7th, you have the ability to switch Medicare Part D drug plans. You can:

- Join a Medicare Prescription Drug Plan (PDP).
- Switch from one Medicare PDP to another Medicare PDP.
- Drop your prescription drug coverage.

If you switch, benefits for coverage become effective January 1, 2014.

LOW INCOME SUBSIDY (LIS)

Individuals who have limited income and resources may qualify for Extra Help from Medicare to cover Part D premiums and out-of-pocket costs. To qualify:

- You must be entitled to Medicare Part A or you are enrolled in Medicare Part B.

- You must also live in one of the 50 states or the District of Columbia.
- If you are single and your income is less than $17,235 and have resources of less than $13,300
- If married and your income is less than $23,265 and have resources of less than $26,580.

In some cases Medicare will consider your assets as well as your income to determine if you are eligible for Extra Help. Assets counted include:

- Cash (checking and savings).
- CDs (certificates of deposit).
- Retirement accounts (IRAs and 401(k)s).
- Stocks, bonds and mutual funds.
- Promissory notes.
- Property which can be converted to cash within 20 days.
- Mortgages.
- Life insurance policies.

Assets not counted include:

- Your primary home.
- Your primary car.
- Burial plots or agreements.
- Funds set aside for burial expenses (up to $1,500).

In addition to LIS, there are pharmaceutical manufacturers who assist low income individuals with reduced or no drug costs.

USING MEDICARE DRUG COVERAGE

The first time you use your new Medicare prescription drug plan you should come to your pharmacy with:

- Your red, white, and blue Medicare card.
- A photo ID (such as a state driver's license or passport).
- Your plan membership card.

If you have both Medicare and Medicaid or qualify for Extra Help with drug plan costs you should also bring proof of your enrollment in Medicaid or proof that you qualify for extra assistance. Within 5 weeks, or possible sooner, after the plan gets your completed application you should get a welcome package from your drug plan provider with your membership card. If you need to go to the pharmacy before your membership card arrives you can use any of the following as proof of membership:

- A letter from the plan that includes your membership information. You should receive this letter within 2 weeks after the plan gets your completed application.
- An enrollment confirmation number you got from the plan, the plan name and phone number.
- A temporary card you may be able to print from Medicare.gov.

Your pharmacist may be able to get your drug plan information if you provide your Medicare number or the last 4 digits of your Social Security number if you don't have any of the items listed above. Otherwise you may have to pay out-of-pocket for your prescriptions. Save your receipts and contact your plan to get your money back.

LIVING IN FLORIDA

This section is designed for readers who live in the state of Florida. As a licensed insurance agent in Florida I am appointed with a number of health insurance companies which offer Medicare Prescription Drug Part D (PDP) plans. While space doesn't permit me to go into all the specifics of each type of plan offered by those insurance companies, I can provide some generalizations about the free-standing PDPs in Florida. What follows is not a solicitation for the purchase of a Medicare Prescription Drug Plan but is meant for general and educational information only. *This may or may not be representative of the costs you see and benefits offered in states other than Florida.* In Florida the insurance companies will use names such as value, saver plus, choice, preferred, enhanced, secure and premier among others, attached to their brands to market their different plans to members and consumers.

Medicare Part D Plan Document

We're going to provide a brief synopsis of what a Medicare Prescription Drug Part D plan document will have in it. These plan documents are also referred to as an Enrollment Kit. The package will usually have:

- Plan Pricing.

- Preferred Pharmacy Network.
- Enrollment Form.
- Summary of Benefits.
- CMS Star Rating Designation.
- Scope of Appointment (SOA) Form.
- Outbound Enrollment and Verification (OEV).

Since original Medicare does not cover most drugs the *Summary of Benefits* section in a PDP plan document will compare premium costs, deductibles, retail pharmacy drug tier level copays and mail order drug tier level copays for the different PDPs which that particular insurance company may offer. Packages from each insurance company, containing all plan materials, will probably be different when opened.

Monthly Plan Premiums

In Florida, most insurance companies will offer their PDPs with the same premium costs statewide. For 2014 many insurance companies are offering multiple prescription drug plans which have a range of monthly premiums. What this means is the cost for Plan A is the same throughout the state. Plan B may have different costs but it is the same throughout the state also. This is different from what we saw with Medicare Advantage Plans and Medicare Supplement Plans in which costs and/or benefits are based on the county you live in. What are key considerations you should consider when comparing different plans:

- How much are the monthly premiums?
- What is the annual deductible?
- What are the copayments?

- Is there any coinsurance?
- What are my total out-of-pocket expenses?
- Are all of my prescriptions covered?
- Which pharmacies can I use?

For 2014, the monthly premiums for most of these plans can vary considerable. One plan was as low as $12.60/month. The highest I saw was $174.70/month. Most plans are between $50 and $70/month. That's a wide range of potential premium costs each month for a stand-alone PDP. There are 5 pharmacy tiers available in PDPs and not all plans will necessarily cover all 5 pharmacy tiers.

Coverage Deductibles and Copays

Plans with the lowest monthly premiums will usually have the $310 deductible (discussed earlier in the chapter) which you need to first meet before the plan begins covering prescriptions. These plans will usually cover the most commonly used generic drugs. Those at the higher price range usually don't have a deductible connected with the plan and will usually have a more extensive drug list and cover all 5 pharmacy tiers.

Copays for Tier 1 prescription drugs can range from as low as $0 to as high as $5 for each medication for preferred networks and up to $7 for non-preferred networks depending on the plan. Copays for Tier 2 medications can range from $2 to as high as $5 for preferred networks and up to $10 for non-preferred networks. Copays for Tier 3 prescription medications can range from $25 to as high as $50 for preferred networks and up to $55 for non-preferred networks. Tier 4 medications can have copays from $45 to as

141

high as $95 for preferred networks and up to $100 for non-preferred networks. There are some plans which have coinsurance for Tier 4 medications up to 50%. Most Tier 5 drugs have coinsurance payments between 25% and 40% for either preferred or non-preferred pharmacy networks. The costs described above are for a 1 month supply. Each plan usually has a mail order option for 60 day and 90 day supplies which afford you greater savings in your prescription drug costs.

As a consumer turning 65, you need to understand what you're paying for your prescription medications, what pharmacy tiers the drugs fall into and the number of times you need to refill them throughout the year to be able to compare which plan might be most cost effective for you.

As I've said before, be careful when you hear the terms free or $0 used. There's nothing wrong with them as long as you fully understand the context in how they are used and what that means. PDPs can have deductibles, copays and coinsurance, depending on which pharmacy tier the specific prescription medication falls in. Not all prescription medications may be covered by every plan. As we have seen costs for PDPs in Florida are all over the map so it definitely pays to do your homework before you purchase a plan. Be patient, don't rush, read everything carefully and be thoughtful when making your decision.

Make a list of all your current prescription drugs. Next, look at the plans available in your service area. Compare cost, coverage and customer service. Decide and then chose the plan that's best for you based on your needs assessment and income levels.

CHAPTER NINE

MEDICARE SUPPLEMENT/MEDIGAP PLANS

Original Medicare pays for much but not all hospitalization, medical services and supplies. Medicare typically pays for about 80% of hospitalization and medical services leaving you with 20% of the cost still to pay. Remember - there is no cap on that 20% you're responsible for. With a $100,000 medical event you could still be responsible for $20,000 with just original Medicare. This is the key downside to just having original Medicare. With Medicare Advantage plans there is a yearly maximum out-of-pocket expense limit, though this could still leave you with an expense between $5,000 and $8,000. In addition, Medicare Advantage plans also have copays and coinsurance you must pay each time you visit your physicians or hospital.

Medicare Supplement/Medigap plans fill in the gaps that original Medicare doesn't cover. These plans are also called Med Supp plans. The plans are sold by private health insurance companies and can help pay some or all of the health care costs not covered by Medicare. These costs could include some or all copays, coinsurance and deductibles not covered by Medicare. You must be enrolled in original Medicare Part A **and** Part B. Medicare does not pay any of the costs for you to get a Med Supp policy. **Thus, you will also pay a monthly premium for your Med Supp policy in addition to your monthly premium Medicare Part B.** Med Supp policies usually don't cover long-term care, vision or dental care, hearing aids, eyeglasses or private-duty nursing.

Med Supp policies sold after January 1, 2006, are not allowed to include prescription drug coverage. If you want a prescription drug coverage plan you can join a Medicare PDP, which was discussed in the previous chapter. If you don't enroll when first eligible, re-read Chapter 4 to understand what, if any penalties, you may be subject to should you decide to enroll at a later date. These penalties could be significant.

Like Medicare Advantage, a Med Supp policy covers only one person. Spouses must buy separate policies. If you're under 65 and have Medicare because of a disability or ESRD, you might not be able to buy a Med Supp policy until you turn 65. Federal law doesn't require insurance companies to sell Med Supp policies to individuals under 65. However, some states may require the insurance company to offers plans to those who are under 65 and disabled. It's important to compare Med Supp policies since the costs can vary and may go up as you get older. Some states limit Med Supp costs. See Chapter 4 for enrollment specifics regarding Med Supp plans.

MEDICARE SUPPLEMENT PLAN TYPES

Every Med Supp policy must follow federal and state laws designed to protect you and it must be clearly identified as Medicare Supplement Insurance. Health insurance companies can only sell you a "standardized" policy identified in most states by letters A–N. Any standardized Med Supp policy is guaranteed renewable even if you have health problems. In other words, the insurance company can't cancel your policy as long as you pay the premiums.

Health insurance companies selling Med Supp policies are required to make Plan A available. If they offer any other Med Supp plans they must also offer either the Plan C or Plan F. Plans D and G, effective on or after June 1, 2010, have different benefits than D or G Plans bought before June 1, 2010. Plans E, H, I, and J are no longer available to buy but if you already have one of those policies you can keep it. All policies offer the same basic benefits but some may offer additional benefits. You can choose which one best meets your needs for coverage and benefits.

In Figure 9.1, on the next page, the table illustrates the basic information about the different benefits that the various Med Supp plans cover. If a check mark appears the plan covers the described benefit 100%. If a percentage appears the plan covers that percentage of the benefit.

Figure 9.1 Comparison of Medicare Supplement/Medigap Plan Types

Medigap Benefits	Medigap Plans									
	A	B	C	D	F*	G	K	L	M	N
Medicare Part A Coinsurance and hospital costs up to an additional 365 days after Medicare benefits are used up	✓	✓	✓	✓	✓	✓	✓	✓	✓	✓
Medicare Part B Coinsurance or Copayment	✓	✓	✓	✓	✓	✓	50%	75%	✓	✓***
Blood (First 3 Pints)	✓	✓	✓	✓	✓	✓	50%	75%	✓	✓
Part A Hospice Care Coinsurance or Copayment	✓	✓	✓	✓	✓	✓	50%	75%	✓	✓
Skilled Nursing Facility Care Coinsurance			✓	✓	✓	✓	50%	75%	✓	✓
Medicare Part A Deductible		✓	✓	✓	✓	✓	50%	75%	50%	✓
Medicare Part B Deductible			✓		✓					
Medicare Part B Excess Charges					✓	✓				
Foreign Travel Emergency (Up to Plan Limits)			✓	✓	✓	✓			✓	✓

Out-of-Pocket Limit**	
$4,660	$2,330

*Plan F also offers a high-deductible plan. If you choose this option, this means you must pay for Medicare-covered costs up to the deductible amount of $2,070 in 2012 before your Medigap plan pays anything.

**After you meet your out-of-pocket yearly limit and your yearly Part B deductible ($140 in 2012), the Medigap plan pays 100% of covered services for the rest of the calendar year.

***Plan N pays 100% of the Part B coinsurance, except for a copayment of up to $20 for some office visits and up to a $50 copayment for emergency room visits that don't result in an inpatient admission.

Courtesy: Centers for Medicare & Medicaid Services; 2013 Choosing a Medigap Policy

In some states you may be able to buy another type of Med Supp policy called Medicare SELECT. It is a plan which requires you to use specific hospitals, and in some cases, specific doctors or other health care providers to get full coverage, except in the case of an emergency. These policies, if available to you, generally cost less than other Med Supp plans. **However, if you don't use the Medicare SELECT health care providers you will have to pay some or all of what Medicare doesn't cover**. If you buy a Medicare SELECT policy you have the right to change your mind within 12 months and switch to a standard Med Supp policy.

GUARANTEED ISSUE RIGHTS (GIRs)

Guaranteed issue rights are also known as Med Supp protection. If you aren't within the Med Supp Open Enrollment Period, there are several situations in which you still have a guaranteed right to buy a Med Supp policy if you're 65 or older. You have a GIR when you have other health care coverage that changes in some way, such as when you lose other health care coverage.

You have a GIR if:

- You're in a Medicare Advantage plan and your plan is leaving Medicare or stops giving care in your area or you move out of the plan's service area. You have the right to purchase Med Supp plans A, B, C, F, K or L that's sold in your state by any insurance company. You must or can apply **as early as 60 calendar days before the date your health coverage will end but no later than 63 calendar days after your**

147

coverage ends. However, you only have this right if you switch back to original Medicare rather than joining another Medicare Advantage plan.

- You have original Medicare and an employer group health plan (including retiree or COBRA coverage) or union coverage that pays after Medicare pays and the plan is ending. You have the right to purchase Med Supp plans A, B, C, F, K, or L that's sold in your state by any insurance company. If you have COBRA you can purchase a Med Supp plan right away or wait until the COBRA coverage ends. You must or can apply **no later than 63 calendar days after the latest** of these three dates: (1) date coverage ends, (2) date on the notice you get telling you that coverage is ending or (3) date on a claim denial if this is the only way you knew you're coverage ended.

- You have original Medicare and a Medicare SELECT plan and you move out of the SELECT plan's service area. You have the right to purchase Med Supp plans A, B, C, F, K, or L that's sold in your state by any insurance company. You must or can apply **as early as 60 calendar days before** the date your Medicare SELECT coverage will end but **no later than 63 calendar days** after your Medicare SELECT coverage ends.

Still, in other cases you have a trial right to try a Medicare Advantage plan and still buy a Med Supp plan if you change your mind. You have a trial right if:

- You joined a Medicare Advantage plan when you were first eligible for Medicare Part A at 65 and within the first year you decide you want to switch to original Medicare. You have the right to purchase any Med Supp policy that's sold in your state by any insurance company. You must or can apply **as early as 60 calendar days before the date your health coverage will end but no later than 63 calendar days after your coverage ends.**
- You dropped a Med Supp policy to join a Medicare Advantage plan for the first time and have been in the plan for less than a year and want to switch back. If your former Med Supp policy isn't available you have the right to purchase Med Supp plans A, B, C, F, K, or L that's sold in your state by any insurance company. You must or can apply **as early as 60 calendar days before the date your health coverage will end but no later than 63 calendar days after** your coverage ends.
- Your Med Supp insurance company goes bankrupt and you lose your coverage or your Med Supp policy coverage otherwise ends through no fault of your own. You have the right to purchase Med Supp plans A, B, C, F, K, or L that's sold in your state by any insurance company. You must or can apply **no later than 63 calendar days after your coverage ends.**
- You leave a Medicare Advantage plan or drop your Med Supp policy because the insurance company hasn't followed the rules or it misled you. You have the right to purchase Med Supp plans A, B, C, F, K, or L that's sold in your state

149

by any insurance company. You must or can apply **no later than 63 calendar days after your coverage ends.**

If you have a guaranteed issue right to buy a Med Supp policy you should keep the following;

- Copies of any letters, notices, emails and/or claim denials which have your name on them as proof of your coverage being terminated.
- Keep the postmarked envelopes these letters come in as proof of when it was mailed. The insurance company may want to see copies with your submitted Medigap application to prove you have a GIR.

MEDICARE SUPPLEMENT/MEDIGAP COVERAGE IN MASSACHUSETTS, MINNESOTA AND WISCONSIN

For 2014, Medicare Supplement/Medigap plans which are available in Massachusetts, Minnesota and Wisconsin are standardized in a different way. There are 2 plans in Massachusetts; Minnesota has 2 plans with mandatory riders while Wisconsin has 1 plan with optional riders.

Massachusetts

For inpatient hospital care the plans cover Medicare Part A coinsurance plus coverage for 365 additional days after Medicare coverage ends. Also covered is Medicare Part B coinsurance, the first 3 pints of blood each year and the Part A hospice coinsurance or copay.

150

In Massachusetts the two available plans consist of a core and a standardized plan. Figure 9.2 below illustrates the benefits available in both plans.

Figure 9.2 Massachusetts Medigap Plan

Medigap Benefits	Core Plan	Supplement 1 Plan
Basic Benefits	✓	✓
Medicare Part A: Inpatient Hospital Deductible		✓
Medicare Part A: Skilled Nursing Facility Coinsurance		✓
Medicare Part B: Deductible		✓
Foreign Travel Emergency		✓
Inpatient Days in Mental Health Hospitals	60 days per calendar year	120 days per benefit year
State-Mandated Benefits (Annual Pap tests and mammograms. Check your plan for other state-mandated benefits.)	✓	✓

Courtesy: Centers for Medicare & Medicaid Services;
2013 Choosing a Medigap Policy

Minnesota

For inpatient hospital care the plans cover the Medicare Part A coinsurance. Also covered is the Medicare Part B coinsurance, the first 3 pints of blood each year and the Part A hospice and respite cost sharing, and Part A and Part B home health services and supplies cost sharing. In Minnesota, the 2 plans available are a Basic Plan and an Extended Plan. There are four mandatory riders which can be added to either plan. An individual can choose one or all four.

151

Figure 9.3 below illustrates the 2 plans and the mandatory riders which are available.

Figure 9.3 Minnesota Medigap Plan

Medigap Benefits	Basic Plan	Extended Basic Plan	Mandatory Riders
Basic Benefits	✓	✓	Insurance companies can offer four additional riders that can be added to a Basic Plan. You may choose any one or all of the following riders to design a Medigap policy that meets your needs:
Medicare Part A: Inpatient Hospital Deductible		✓	
Medicare Part A: Skilled Nursing Facility (SNF) Coinsurance	✓ (Provides 100 days of SNF care)	✓ (Provides 120 days of SNF care)	
Medicare Part B: Deductible		✓	
Foreign Travel Emergency	80%	80%*	
Outpatient Mental Health	50%	50%	• Medicare Part A: Inpatient Hospital Deductible
Usual and Customary Fees		80%*	
Medicare-covered Preventive Care	✓	✓	
Physical Therapy	20%	20%	• Medicare Part B: Deductible
Coverage while in a Foreign Country		80%*	• Usual and Customary Fees
State-mandated Benefits (Diabetic equipment and supplies, routine cancer screening, reconstructive surgery, and immunizations)	✓	✓	• Non-Medicare Preventive Care

Courtesy: Centers for Medicare & Medicaid Services;
2013 Choosing a Medigap Policy

Wisconsin

For inpatient hospital care the plan covers the Medicare Part A coinsurance. Also covered is the Medicare Part B coinsurance, the first 3 pints of blood each year and the Part A hospice coinsurance or copay. In Wisconsin, there is 1 Basic Plan with optional riders which can be purchased. Figure 9.4 below illustrates the plan and available optional riders.

Figure 9.4 Wisconsin Medigap Plan

Medigap Benefits	Basic Plan	Optional Riders
Basic Benefits	✓	Insurance companies are allowed to offer the following additional riders to a Medigap policy:
Medicare Part A: Skilled Nursing Facility Coinsurance	✓	• Part A Deductible
Inpatient Mental Health Coverage	175 days per lifetime in addition to Medicare's benefit	• Additional Home Health Care (365 visits including those paid by Medicare)
Home Health Care	40 visits in addition to those paid by Medicare	• Part B Deductible
		• Part B Excess Charges
State Mandated Benefits	✓	• Foreign Travel Emergency
		• 50% Part A Deductible
		• Part B Copayment or Coinsurance

Courtesy: Centers for Medicare & Medicaid Services;
2013 Choosing a Medigap Policy

PREMIUM COSTS

If you're turning 65 the monthly premium costs for these plans can range from around $100 to as much as $300 each month, depending on whether you use tobacco or not. You'll also want to know if premiums can increase with your age. A high-end Med Supp plan will protect you more than a Medicare Advantage plan but it will also cost you a lot more. The deductibles can vary by insurance provider. Benefits are standardized and coded by a letter so you can compare one insurance provider's C plan with that of another insurance provider's C plan. If you buy a Med Supp plan within the first six months of going on original Medicare Part B, your Med Supp Open Enrollment Period, you can't be turned down or charged more because of your health. If you wait until after your Open Enrollment Period the insurance company will use medical underwriting requirements and there is no guarantee the insurance company will sell you a Med Supp policy if you don't meet the necessary medical requirements.

How do insurance companies set premiums for their Med Supp policies? Med Supp policies can be priced in three ways to determine premiums:

- *Community-No Age Rated:* Generally the same monthly premium is charged to everyone in a designated area that has the policy regardless of age. Your premium isn't based on your age but may go up because of inflation and other factors but not because off your age.
- *Issue-age Rated:* Your premium is based on the age you are when you purchase the policy. Premiums are thus lower for individuals who buy at a younger age and won't change as you get older. As with community rated, premiums can go up because of factors other than your age like inflation.

- *Attained-age Rated:* Your premium is based on your current or attained age and will go up as you get older. Premiums are low for younger buyers but go up as you get older. This rating process may be the least expensive in the beginning but could end up being the most expensive based on how old you get and other factors such as inflation.

It's important to understand this because the way they set premiums determines how much you pay now and in the future. This is critical in incorporating your future premiums into your financial plan. Other factors such as geographical rating, medical underwriting, discounts and future inflation can also affect the amounts of your premiums.

SWITCHING PLANS

Some reasons for switching Med Supp policies might include:

- Paying for benefits you don't need.
- You now need more benefits than your current plan provides.
- Your policy has the right benefits but you want to change health care insurance companies.
- Your policy has the right benefits but you want to find a policy that's less expensive.

In most cases, under federal law, you won't have a right to switch Med Supp policies unless you're within **your** 6-month Med Supp Open Enrollment Period or are eligible under a specific circumstance for guaranteed issue rights. However, some states may have more generous requirements or the health insurance company may be willing to sell you a different policy. **If you do decide to make a switch make sure you compare both premiums and benefits and also ask about medical underwriting and pre-existing conditions.**

Currently Enrolled in a Medicare Supplement Plan

If you purchased your Med Supp policy before 2010 it may offer coverage that isn't available in a newer Med Supp policy. However, Med Supp policies bought before 1992 might not be guaranteed renewable and may have bigger premium increases than newer, standardized Med Supp policies currently being sold. If you've had your existing Med Supp policy for less than six months and switch, the insurance company may be able to make you wait up to six months for coverage of a pre-existing condition.

If you decide to switch, don't cancel your first Med Supp policy until you have decided to keep the second Med Supp policy. On the application for the new Med Supp policy you will have to promise that you will cancel your first Med Supp policy. Once you're new policy is issued you have 30 days to decide if you want to keep the new Med Supp policy. This is called your free look period. The 30-day free look period starts when you actually receive your new Med Supp policy. **Should you decide to keep the new policy you will need to pay both premiums for one month to keep both policies enforce while you decide.** Once you cancel the policy you can't get it back.

Currently Enrolled in a Medicare Advantage Plan

If you have a Medicare Advantage plan now it's illegal for anyone to sell you a Med Supp policy unless you're switching back to original Medicare. If you're enrolling in a Medicare Advantage plan for the first time and you aren't happy with the plan you will have special rights to buy a Med Supp policy if you return to original Medicare within 12 months of enrolling. If you had a Med Supp policy before you joined you may be able to get the same policy back if the insurance company still sells it. If it isn't available you can buy another Med Supp policy. The Med Supp policy can no longer have prescription drug coverage even if you had it before but you may be able to join a Medicare Prescription Drug plan. If you joined a Medicare Advantage Plan when you were first eligible for Medicare you can choose from any Med Supp policy.

LIVING IN FLORIDA

This section is designed for readers of the book who live in the state of Florida. As a licensed insurance agent in Florida I am appointed with a number of health insurance companies which offer Medicare Supplement plans. While space doesn't permit me to go into all the specifics of each plan letter offered by those insurance companies, I can provide some generalizations about Medicare Supplement plans in Florida. What follows is not a solicitation for the purchase of a Medicare Supplement plan but is meant for general and educational information only. *This may or may not be representative of the costs and benefits offered in states other than Florida.*

Medicare Supplement Plan Document

We're going to provide a brief synopsis of what a Medicare Supplement plan document will have in it. These plan documents are also referred to as an Enrollment Kit. The package will usually have:

- Premium Rates for Plans Offered.
- Eligibility Requirements.
- Benefits Covered.
- Enrollment Forms.
- Payment Options.

Premiums

In Florida, many insurance companies will use 3 criteria to base their plan premiums on. (1) The insurance company may group zip codes into a number of different areas. Which zip code you live in will determine which area you are in and thus the premium costs for enrolling in a specific Medicare Supplement plan, (2) some companies will also base their premiums on whether or not you are a tobacco user. Premiums will be lower for non-tobacco users and (3) the insurance company incorporates specific age brackets which they use at the time of enrollment in the plan. The older you are at the time of enrollment the higher your monthly premiums will be. Premiums are more expensive in south Florida than they are in either central or northern Florida. Effective January 1, 2014, premiums are rising for some Medicare Supplement plans, on average, by 2.5% to 3.0% for non-select plans and as much as 10% for select plans being offered in Florida.

The premiums illustrated for the plans below are for **2014**. **Plan F** is considered the "Cadillac Plan" or BMW, Mercedes, etc. by many. As you can see from Figure 6.1 earlier, it covers just about everything and will also cost the most in terms of monthly premiums. For a non-tobacco user, at age 65 monthly premiums could be between $173 and $261. For ages 66-69, monthly premiums could increase to between $187 and $283. Over age 80 and over, premiums could increase to between $249 and $375 each month. If you're turning 65, you could expect to pay slightly less than $2,100 to slightly more than $3,100 in premiums for the year for complete coverage.

For a tobacco user, at age 65, monthly premiums could be between $190 and $288. For ages 66-69, monthly premiums could increase to between $206 and $312. For age 80 and over, premiums could increase to between $273 and $413 each month. If you're turning 65, and a tobacco user, you could expect to pay slightly less than $2,300 to just over $3,450 in premiums for the year for complete coverage.

Plan A is considered your basic Medicare Supplement plan. Every insurance company which offers Med Supp plans must offer a Plan A. It covers basic benefits plus 100% of the Part B coinsurance. For a non-tobacco user, at age 65, monthly premiums could be between $126 and $191. For ages 66-69, monthly premiums could increase to between $136 and $206. Age 80 and over, premiums could increase to between $181 and $274 each month. If you're turning 65, you could expect to pay slightly more than $1,500 in premiums to just under $2,300 in premiums for the year for basic coverage.

For a tobacco user, at age 65, monthly premiums could be between $138 and $210. For ages 66-69, monthly premiums could increase to between $150 and $227. For age 80 and over, premiums could increase to between $199 and $301 each month for basic coverage. If you're turning 65, and a tobacco user, you could expect to pay from just over $1,650 to slightly more than $2,500 in premiums for the year for basic coverage.

Now let's take a look at one more plan that is in the middle in terms of costs and benefits covered. **Plan K** has some shared costs as you can see from Figure 6.1. While hospitalization and preventive care are paid at 100%, other basic benefits are covered at 50%. SNF has 50% coinsurance as does the Part A deductible. While Plans F and A have no out-of-pocket limits, Plan K does. These out-of pocket limits could be as high as $4,800 each year. As you might expect, this plan also has lower monthly premiums than the previous two.

For a non-tobacco user, at age 65, monthly premiums could be between $69 and $104. For ages 66-69, monthly premiums could increase to between $74 and $113. At age 80 and over, premiums could increase to between $99 and $149 each month. If you're turning 65, you could expect to pay from $828 to nearly $1,250 in premiums for the year for shared coverage with an out-of-pocket limit.

For a tobacco user, at age 65, monthly premiums could be between $75 and $115. For ages 66-69, monthly premiums could increase to between $81 and $124. At age 80 and over, premiums could increase to between $108 and $164 each month. If you're turning 65, and a tobacco user, you could expect to pay from

$900 to nearly $1,400 in premiums for the year for shared coverage with an out-of pocket limit.

Benefits Covered

A Med Supp plan document doesn't have a summary of benefits section like a Medicare Advantage plan but it does outline what Medicare pays, what the Med Supp plan pays and what you pay for services incurred. Some Med Supp plans will offer additional member benefits which can include fitness memberships, vision discounts and access to registered nursing professional over the telephone.

FINAL THOUGHTS ON MEDICARE SUPPLEMENT/MEDIGAP PLANS

As you shop for a policy be sure you're comparing apples to apples. Compare Plan A from one company with Plan A from another company. Different insurance companies may charge different premiums for the same exact policy. Also ask about the history of premium changes recently. Many times consumers may feel confused by all the different plans and premiums. You need to take a step back and think about you current health status and match that up with the plan that best suits your health needs and what your monthly budget will allow.

Visit www.medicare.gov/publications to view the booklet, *2013 Choosing a Medigap Policy: A Guide to Health Insurance for People with Medicare.* You can also call 1-800-MEDICARE (1-800-633-4227) to find out if a copy can be mailed to you. TTY users should call 1-877-486-2048.

161

"Doctors cannot afford to provide care at the rate of reimbursement that Medicare insists that they accept."

Nan Hayworth
Republican U.S. House of Representatives -
New York's 19th Congressional District
Physician

CHAPTER TEN

CHOICES FOR LONG-TERM CARE

If you don't meet all the requirements for Medicaid, what is your plan for long-term care should the need arise? **Medicare is not going to cover what you're going to need, if you need it.** Many individuals may not need long-term care (LTC) until they reach their 70s, 80s or 90s. However, if you wait that long until you actually need it, the costs involved in obtaining the needed coverage may be cost prohibitive or you may not even be able to qualify for LTC coverage. This doesn't even consider the possibility of a sudden event occurring much earlier in life requiring LTC. LTC is a health issue that should be planned for in advance because of the escalating costs involved as you get older and potentially less healthy.

Like the Medicare health plans, LTC insurance can vary from state to state; in what is sold, the coverage and benefits the policy provides and the premiums you pay. We're going to cover LTC in general, solutions for getting LTC other than with insurance and LTC insurance. We'll conclude with a look at the issues facing LTC insurance right now in wake of the Great Financial Crisis and a Federal Reserve that has now implemented a zero-rate monetary policy going on nearly 5 years. This has severely impacted the yields insurance companies, who provide LTC insurance, can obtain on their fixed income portfolios which account for up to 60% of their revenues to pay benefits. The last five years have brought seismic changes to this industry.

LONG-TERM CARE SURVEYS

Let's take a look at a few surveys which were done within the past two years on attitudes, beliefs and behavior regarding long-term care and the need for it. Surveys have a value in accessing perception, at a specific point in time, even though they may present conflicting conclusions depending on who conducted them.

In the fall of 2012, John Hancock released its *Study of Consumer Behavior*, prepared by The Forbes Consulting Group, which was an online survey of 305 individuals aged 45-65 who had household incomes greater than $70,000 and investable assets of over $100,000. Of those who indicated they would NOT consider purchasing a LTC policy, 74% cited cost of the policy as the primary reason. Major reasons for considering purchasing an LTC policy pertained to the need for planning and to protect one's family. LTC insurance as an important part of financial planning for retirement was identified by 77% of respondent versus only 23% who would consider purchasing because of a personal experience. Those who indicated their primary goal in considering purchase was to avoid becoming a burden to their family was identified by 62% of respondents. Only 38% would buy to retain control over their care. Those who said their primary goal for purchasing was to protect their family was 54% while only 46% indicated their goal was to protect their assets. An insurance carrier's reputation and financial strength was also found to be a critical factor in purchasing LTC insurance.

In November 2012, a study from Northwestern Mutual, *The Long-Term Care Awareness Study*, was conducted by Harris Interactive and surveyed 2,516 adults. The study found that a third haven't factored their LTC needs into their retirement planning. Nearly a quarter aren't sure how they'll address LTC needs and 8% say they're not going to address them at all. This is despite the fact that 55% of respondents think they will need LTC at some point in their lives. The study also found less than half of the respondents felt financially prepared to live beyond age 75 and only 38% say they are prepared to live beyond 85.

In February 2013, Nationwide Financial released a survey regarding perceptions of long-term care among baby boomers. Their survey included 813 respondents, 50 years of age and older and who have at least $150,000 in annual income or in investible assets. Most respondents think of long-term care as nursing home care or assisted living. The fact: nearly half of LTC is done in the home by a home health-care worker or is adult day care. When asked to estimate how much nursing home care will cost a year in 2030, respondents estimated an average of $111,507. This is less than half the actual estimated costs, which are projected to be $265,000 a year. In 2013 it is currently about $67,000 a year. According to John Carter, president and chief operating officer of retirement plans for Nationwide Financial, nursing home costs have increased more than 4% annually since 1974. Other findings include those aged 50 or older who have not retired believe they will live an average of only 20.7 years in retirement, while those already in retirement believe they will live 27.1 years in retirement. Most respondents indicated they have a plan for their finances in retirement but 57% admitted they had not taken long-term care costs into consideration.

U.S. Trust, a unit of Bank of America, surveyed 711 high-net worth individuals with over $3 million in investable assets. LTC costs were unseen risks which were not well reflected in the financial planning process. Even though 47% of the respondents had created a financial plan to address LTC needs they and their spouse/partner might need; only 18% had a financial plan that accounts for their parents' LTC costs. Of these respondents, 46% indicated they have provided substantial financial support to adult family members with 69% indicating they do not have a financial plan which accounts for the financial needs of any of these other adult family members.

NO PRIOR EXPERIENCE

The real perception for most individuals in their 40s, 50s and even into their 60s is, *"nothing is going to happen to me so why would I want to pay for a product I'll never need."* Most individuals feel this way because they have no prior experience. By no prior experience I mean they have never been **directly** involved as the **primary caregiver**, NOT to be confused with the primary earner. Knowing someone who has acted in this capacity or even another individual within your extended family does not count. Once you have gained prior experience you now understand the emotional, physical and financial consequences the event poses to the family. You have experienced the fear. Those you love have no choice but to set aside their lives to provide assistance and/or supervision on a 24 hour basis.

Extended care usually results from two impairments. One is physical; where a chronic medical condition compromises the individual's ability to get through most of their activities of daily living. The other is cognitive; where there is a measurable decline in intellect. Of claims which are filed, 80-85% of the LTC claims are from the neck up.

How individuals response to the possibility of an unexpected death or disability is based on their role in the family. Whether this is the other spouse or an adult child, some individuals are more emotionally mature than others within the family. **Unlike primary earners' who view the risk of an unexpected death or disability as negligible; primary caregivers view them as events with serious consequences to their ability to continue providing for the day to day needs of the family.** Providing care to those who are chronically ill often makes a healthy caregiver chronically ill. These situations can tear them apart both physically and emotionally.

In October 2013, Genworth Financial released a report, *Beyond Dollars: A Way Forward*, which surveyed more than 1,200 caregivers and recipients receiving LTC. Those who identified themselves as caregivers; more than 50% said they had lost income because of those responsibilities. Thirty-eight percent of caregivers indicated they could have avoided a lot of stress if they had started planning for care earlier while 35% of recipients agreed. Many of those who participated said they made a mistake by not purchasing LTC insurance. Almost 60% of respondents, who didn't have a LTC policy, wished they had purchased one. Of those, nearly 60% felt it would have been easier on their finances and would have put less strain on their family. According to the report, Genworth believes families could save almost $11,000 per year on out-of-pocket expenses for LTC if they started planning earlier.

The need for LTC is a very real potential risk. In many ways LTC insurance is no different than life insurance, homeowners insurance or car insurance. Pay the premiums now and transfer the risk to an insurance company, which covers you and pays you benefits should you need them. Or you don't pay the premiums and pray you never need the coverage. If you do you're probably screwed if you don't have the cash reserves available. Your retirement plan then implodes and you're suddenly faced with a radically different lifestyle ahead of you than what you had expected for your later years. Not an enjoyable scenario.

LTC OVERVIEW

Despite medical improvements and advances in pharmacology, health conditions for a majority of the U.S. population are getting worse. As the population ages and life expectancies increase, there is an increased risk for the need for long-term care. According to the CMS, almost 70% of individuals aged 65 can expect to eventually require some level of services and support to meet personal care needs over an extended period of time. Those who reach 65 will likely have a 40% chance of entering a nursing home. About 10% of the individuals who enter a nursing home will stay there five years or more.

According to the American Association for Long-Term Care Insurance (AALTCI), in 2013, LTC insurers paid $7.5 billion in long-term care insurance benefits to approximately 273,000 individuals, an increase of 13%. Claimants rose 3% as well over 2012. Insurers paid $6.6 billion to some 264,000 policyholders in 2012. **The most common reasons for claims were Alzheimer's disease, stroke, arthritis and cancer.** In-home care accounted for about half of all new LTC insurance claims and two-thirds of benefit recipients were women. In a separate report released by the AALTCI, in August 2013, it was estimated insurers will pay $15 billion by 2023 and $34 billion by 2033 in LTC benefits when today's 60 year olds, in 2014, reach their 80s.

In their 2012 annual report, the Life Insurance and Market Research Association reported that about seven million individuals, including about 12% of Americans over age 65, have long-term care coverage.

In an interview with AARP, Susan Collins, a Republican senator from Maine who is on the Senate Aging Committee noted, there are over 5 million Americans who have Alzheimer's disease. There is $200 billion being spent each year caring for these individuals. Medicare and Medicaid account for $142 billion of that being spent and yet only $500 million is invested into researching Alzheimer's.

COST CONCERNS FOR LTC

The costs associated with LTC are quite high. LTC costs generally range from $30,000 - $100,000 per year, depending on the region where you live and the level of care provided. According to the Department of Health and Human Service (HHS), for 2010, the average costs for long-term care in the United States were:

- $205 per day or $6,235 per month for a semi-private room in a nursing home,
- $229 per day or $6,965 per month for a private room in a nursing home,
- $3,293 per month for care in an assisted living facility (for a one-bedroom unit),
- $21 per hour for a home health aide,
- $19 per hour for homemaker services and
- $67 per day for services in an adult day health care center

For comparison since 2010, each year insurance carrier Genworth Financial releases its *Cost of Care Survey*, which looks at home care providers, adult day health care facilities, assisted living facilities and nursing homes. The 2013 survey conducted by CareScout included nearly 15,000 LTC providers from all 50 states and Washington, D.C., divided into 437 regions across the country. The study, in its 10th year, included the following findings in the report:

- Licensed Homemaker Services: National median hourly rate is $18, a 1.39% increase over 2012, with a 5-year annual growth rate of 0.84%.
- Licensed Home Health Aid Services: National median hourly rate is $19, a 2.32% increase over 2012, with a 5-year annual growth rate of 1.0%.
- Adult Day Health Care: National median hourly rate is $65, a 6.56% increase over 2012, with a 5-year annual growth rate of 1.61%.
- Assisted Living Facility (One Bedroom – Single Occupancy): National median monthly rate is $3,450, a 4.55% increase over 2012, with a 5-year annual growth rate of 4.26%. Annual cost: $41,400.
- Nursing Home (Semi-Private Room): National median daily rate is $207, a 3.30% increase over 2012, with a 5-year annual growth rate of 4.22%. Annual cost: $75,555.
- Nursing Home (Private Room): National median daily rate is $230, a 3.60% increase over 2012, with a 5-year annual growth rate of 4.45%. Annual cost: $83,950.

The five year percentage increases listed above represent the compound annual growth rate for surveys conducted from 2008 to 2013. The room you might have had in 2008, at a cost of $67,525 for the year will now cost you $83,950 for the year in 2013; an additional $16,425 per year. The average yearly cost of assisted living is $39,600 for a single room with a single occupant.

According to the Genworth report, the cost of care for Alzheimer's disease, which affects 5.1 million Americans, is projected to rise to $1.2 trillion annually by 2050. This only includes the cost for paid health care, LTC and hospice. The unpaid caregiver's contribution was some 17.5 billion hours of care, valued at more than $216.5 billion for just 2012 alone. Which states had the least expensive (average annual) costs for LTC in 2013?

1. Missouri - $35,645
2. Louisiana - $35,749
3. Alabama - $35,963
4. Oklahoma - $36,936
5. Arkansas - $37,535
6. Texas - $37,751
7. Georgia - $38,713
8. South Carolina - $40,315
9. Iowa - $40,536
10. Kansas - $40,686

States most expensive (average annual) for costs in 2013?

1. Alaska - $103,336
2. Connecticut - $68,983
3. Hawaii - $66,910
4. Massachusetts - $65,212
5. New Jersey - $65,203
6. New York - $59,598

7. Delaware - $59,003
8. Vermont - $58,581
9. New Hampshire - $57,689
10. Maine - $57,628

According to Genworth, though women own about 58% of in-force LTCI policies, they account for nearly 67% of all claims and 71% of all claim dollars paid.

The National Clearinghouse for Long Term Care has a website which gives you a representation of the costs for LTC in various states. Clicking on the link, http://www.longtermcare.gov/LTC/Main_Site/Tools/State_Costs.aspx, takes you to the website which allows you to interact and click on the state where you live to quickly see the costs for long-term care there. Here you can track and project average nationwide costs for home care, adult day care, assisted living facilities and nursing homes. Based on their predicted long-term care needs and lifespans, individuals can estimate inflation-adjusted costs for up to 30 years.

These costs can vary significantly from state to state. For example, the cost of private care in Missouri is about $56,000 a year. In North Carolina it is about $75,000 a year and in New York as much as $120,000 each year. The biggest mistake individuals make in planning for LTC is underestimating these costs.

LTC can be provided at home, in the community, in assisted living or in a nursing home. In 2012, it's estimated about nine million men and women over the age of 65 will need LTC. By 2020, an estimated 12,000,000 individuals may need LTC. Most will be cared for at home. Family and friends are the sole caregivers for 70% of the elderly.

TRIGGERING AN LTC EVENT

LTC constitutes a variety of services which includes medical and non-medical care to individuals who have a chronic illness or disability. Many individuals who require LTC are generally not sick in the traditional sense. Instead they are old and frail and unable to perform some of the basic activities of daily living (ADLs). The six ADLs include:

1. Dressing
2. Bathing
3. Eating
4. Toileting
5. Continence
6. Transferring (getting in and out of a bed or chair)

If you have LTC insurance, you usually become eligible to receive benefits when either of the following events occur and are certified by a Licensed Health Care Practitioner.

- When an illness or accident prevents an individual from performing at least **two activities of daily living** for at least 90 days. Events triggering an LTC event could include heart attack, cancer and other chronic health conditions.
- Substantial supervision to protect yourself from threats and safety due to severe cognitive impairment such as Alzheimer's disease, brain injury, stroke or dementia.

LONG-TERM CARE CHOICES

If you find yourself having to deal with a LTC situation, it helps to have a number of care options available so you can decide which arrangements will work best for you and your family members. Table 10.1, on the following page, provides a summary view of the comparative levels of assistance which are offered with each of the different types of LTC.

Table 10.1 Comparison of LTC Types and Assistance Offered

	Help with activities of daily living	Help with additional services	Help with care needs	Range of Costs
Community Based Services	Yes	Yes	No	Low to Medium
Home Health Care	Yes	Yes	Yes	Low to High
In-Law Apartments	Yes	Yes	No	Low to High
Housing for Aging and Disabled Individuals	Yes	Yes	No	Low to High
Board and Care Homes	Yes	Yes	Yes	Low to High
Assisted Living	Yes	Yes	Yes	Medium to High
Continuing Care Retirement Communities	Yes	Yes	Yes	High
Nursing Homes	Yes	Yes	Yes	High

Courtesy: Medicare; Long Term Care

Each of these options will be discussed in more detail below and we'll provide some insight into how you can get assistance with your long-term care needs.

Community-Based Services

- Adult day care
- Senior centers
- Transportation
- Meals On Wheels
- Telephone reassurance
- Case management

Adult day health care provides social and other related support services in a community-based, protective setting during any part of the day, but is less than 24 hour care.

Home Health Care

- Homemaker services
- Home health aids
- Personal care aide services
- Skilled nursing care
- Respite care
- Medical equipment
- Home repair and modification
- Hospice

Licensed homemaker services provide hands-off care such as helping with cooking and running errands. They are also referred to as personal care assistance or personal care companion. Licensed home health aide services provide hands-on personal care but not medical care in the home. This assistance includes help with daily activities of living such as bathing, dressing, etc.

In-Law Apartments

An in-law apartment is a separate housing arrangement within a single family home or on your lot. It is a complete living space which includes a private bath and kitchen. They are sometimes referred to as a second unit, accessory apartment or accessory dwelling. An in-law apartment may provide a living space for a caretaker or may be rented to provide additional income to you.

Housing for Aging and Disabled Individuals

The Federal government and most states have certain programs which help pay for housing for older people with low or moderate incomes, usually less than $46,000 if single or $53,000 if married. An application must be filled out and many of these programs have a waiting list. Many times these programs also offer assistance with meals and other activities such as housekeeping, shopping and laundry.

Board and Care Homes

This is a group living arrangement which provides help with activities of daily living such as eating, bathing and using the bathroom. These are individuals who typically can't live on their own but do not need nursing home services. This type of care is sometimes called a "group home". In some cases, private long-term care insurance and other types of assistance programs may help pay for this type of living arrangement. Since many of these homes do not receive payments from either Medicare or Medicaid they are not strictly monitored. The monthly charge for this type of arrangement is usually a percentage of your income.

Assisted Living

This group living arrangement provides help with activities of daily living such as eating, bathing, and using the bathroom, taking medicine, and getting to appointments as needed. Residents often live in their own room or apartment within a building or group of buildings and have some or all of their meals together. Social and recreational activities are usually provided. Some assisted living facilities have health services on site. Costs for assisted living facilities can vary widely depending on the size of the living areas, services provided, type of help needed, and where the building is located. Residents usually pay a monthly rent and then pay additional fees for the services that they get. In 2001, the typical cost of living in an assisted living facility ranged from $900 to $3,000 per month. They have increased significantly since then. Costs can be higher in urban areas or in upscale facilities.

Continuing Care Retirement Communities (CCRC)

CCRCs are housing communities which have different levels of care based on your needs. Within the same community, there may be individual homes or apartments for residents who still live on their own, an assisted living facility for people who need some help with daily care, and a nursing home for those who require higher levels of care. Residents are able to move from one level of care to another based on their needs but still stay in the same CCRC.

If you are considering a CCRC, be sure to check the record of its nursing home. Your CCRC contract usually requires you to use the CCRC nursing home if you need this level of care. CCRCs generally charge a large payment before you move in (called an entry fee) and then charge monthly fees. In 2004, entrance fees range from $38,000 to $400,000. Monthly payments can then range from $650 to $3,500 per month.

Nursing Homes

These facilities provide care to those individuals who can't be cared for at either home or in the community 24 hours a day. Nursing homes provide a wide range of personal care and health services. This care generally is to assist people with activities of daily living such as dressing, bathing, and using the bathroom and for individuals who can't take care of themselves due to physical, emotional, or mental problems. **Medicare doesn't pay for this type of care and doesn't pay for most nursing home care.** Some nursing homes may provide skilled care after an injury or hospital stay. Medicare will pay for skilled nursing facility care for a limited period of time if you meet certain conditions.

Generally, Medicare doesn't pay for LTC. Medicare pays only for a medically-necessary skilled nursing facility or home health care. You must meet certain conditions for Medicare to pay for these types of care.

179

Most LTC is custodial care which assists individuals with support services such as dressing, bathing and using the bathroom. **Medicare doesn't pay for custodial care.** When planning for the possibility of a potential LTC event you need to ask the following three questions:

1. Who is going to take care of me when I can't do it myself any longer?
2. Where will I be taken care of?
3. How will I pay for this care?

The questions sound very simple; but the answers and solutions can be extremely complex and filled with significant emotion. These conversations need to take place between spouses and for many baby-boomers with their aging parents.

The cost of long-term care can vary considerably depending on what kind of care you need, where you get care and where you live. To put it simplistically, there are only 4 ways to pay for care if or when you need it.

1. Through family and their financial support.
2. Government programs such as Medicaid if you are in poverty or an indigent.
3. Self-insure – pay for care by depleting your existing financial resources.
4. LTC insurance.

SOLUTIONS OTHER THAN LTC INSURANCE

If the need for LTC arises, remember those three questions we asked earlier in the chapter. Who is going to take care of me, where will I be taken care of and how will I pay for it? Before we look at LTC insurance itself, let's first explore what options are available other than obtaining the insurance for LTC needs.

Family

Traditionally, families usually bore the cost of taking care of older family members when they could no longer maintain their independence. In the early stages for the need of LTC, family assistance may be the only viable option in that it requires the family to minimally assist the older individual. This might include helping with activities such as shopping, home cleaning and cooking. In some cases the family may opt to have the older individual move into the home of younger family members to provide more assistance.

Personal Assets

Many times older individuals don't feel comfortable relying on their children or other family members for support and decide to use their own assets to pay for LTC. One problem that can arise is the assets may not be sufficiently liquid (readily converted to cash without loss) to provide the resources for immediate or long-term needs. They may also significantly deplete their assets, leaving very little left as a legacy to their children or grandchildren.

Medicare

Can provide some benefits for LTC but its restrictive and limited in its scope of care. It covers nursing home and home health care but is limited to skilled nursing care that is rehabilitative. The individual may not be sufficiently ill enough to require skilling nursing care. Medicare will not cover aid associated with ADLs. A physician is required to certify the need for skilled nursing care and any nursing home must be certified by Medicare. Medicare only covers a maximum of 100 days of skilled nursing care and only the first 20 days are covered at 100%.

LTC INSURANCE

Age is not a determining factor in needing long-term care. Being older though definitely increases your risk that you may need it because of a LTC event. According to the U.S. Department of Health and Human Services, in their *Medicare & You, National Medicare Handbook, Centers for Medicare and Medicaid Services, Revised November 2012*, about 70 percent of individuals over age 65 will require at least some type of long-term care services during their lifetime. About 40% of those receiving long-term care today are between 18 and 64. Once a change of health occurs as a result of an LTC event obtaining long-term care insurance may no longer be an available option because of the now pre-existing health condition.

LTC insurance (LTCI) policies are not standardized. LTCI rates are determined by seven main factors:

182

1. The person's age.
2. The daily (or monthly) amount of benefit. Benefit can vary depending on whether it is for nursing home care, assisted living or home care, for example.
3. Duration of how long the benefits are paid. These usually start at 12 months and can last as long as the individual lives. The average is about 5 years. The longer the duration the more costly the premiums.
4. The elimination or waiting period. This is the period of time before benefits are paid. Common periods are 30, 60, 90 and 180-days.
5. Maximum policy benefits once an individual begins receiving benefits.
6. Any inflation protection.
7. Health rating (preferred, standard, sub-standard).

Coverage and caregiver options are most critical when you are evaluating policies. You want as much flexibility as possible. The policy should cover all types of situations whether it is to stay at home or go into a facility. Does the caregiver have to be a licensed caregiver or can it be someone in the family.

Most LTCI companies will offer couples and multi-life discounts on individual policies. Some will define "couples" as not only spouses but also as two people who meet criteria for living together in a committed relationship and sharing basic living expenses. Individuals who probably shouldn't consider purchasing any LTCI are those individuals who:

- May soon begin receiving Medicaid benefits.

- Have limited assets and not being able to afford the premiums over the lifetime of the policy.
- Only source of income is a social security benefit or supplemental security income.

The *National Association of Insurance Commissioners* recommends you should not spend more than 7% of your income on long-term care insurance.

The average age of purchasers has dropped from 68 years in 1990 to 61 years in 2005, and the number of purchasers who are under age 65 has increased significantly. The qualifying process to get a LTC insurance policy is somewhat similar to qualifying for a large life insurance policy. That means you'll most likely have to go through the insurance company's underwriting process. There will be a fairly lengthy application to flush out your current health status. You might also be required to have lab work done to assess your blood chemistry panels. Individuals who have certain health conditions may not qualify for LTCI. Common reasons could include:

- Currently using LTC services.
- Already need help with certain ADLs.
- Have AIDS or AIDS Related Complex (ARC).
- Have Alzheimer's disease or any form of dementia or cognitive dysfunction; a stroke within the past year to two years or a history of strokes.
- Have metastatic cancer.

Once an individual purchases a LTC policy, the language cannot be changed by the insurance company. The policy is usually guaranteed renewable for life and it can never be canceled by the insurance company for health reasons. The only reason it can be canceled is for non-payment of premiums.

Payout Options for Long Term Care Policies

There are several types of LTCI policies which you can buy to insure against needing LTC. These are:

- **Indemnity Policy:** The indemnity policy is used by chronic illness riders. An indemnity or per diem policy pays up to a fixed amount irrespective of what you spend. Benefits are paid in a lump sum. Once received these funds can be used for any purpose.
- **Reimbursement or Expense Incurred Policy:** With a reimbursement policy you choose the benefit amount when you apply for the policy and you are reimbursed for actual expenses for services rendered up to the monthly maximum, which is a fixed dollar amount per day, week or month. Payments are made as expenses are incurred. Any portion of the monthly maximum amount not used is typically available for future benefits.
- **Integrated Policy:** An integrated policy has pooled benefits. This type of policy provides a total dollar amount which may be used for different types of LTC services. There is usually a daily, weekly or monthly dollar limit for your covered LTC expenses.

If you have legally given control of your finances to a care-giver, who is going to be responsible for the payment of your LTC expenses, be sure it is an individual you can trust unequivocally and who will look out for your best interests. There can be a dark side, especially for indemnity policies. Don't make any assumptions just because it may be a family member that you are entrusting. I am aware of situations where caregivers, who were family members, suddenly having a new car appear in their driveway or are taking expensive vacations, which would normally appear out of the realm of their own financial situation.

Benefits and Eligibility

Many LTCI policies have limits on how long or how much the policy will pay. Most policies will pay the costs of your LTC for two to five years. There are some insurance companies which offer policies that will pay your LTC costs for as long as you live, no matter how much it costs, though there are very few companies today that offer such unlimited or lifetime policies. Some insurance companies have a high coverage option, which offer a $1 million lifetime limit.

Most LTCI policies sold today are comprehensive policies. That is the policies generally cover all types of LTC we discussed earlier such as home care, assisted living, adult daycare, respite care, hospice care, nursing home and Alzheimer's facilities. If home care coverage is purchased, LTCI can pay for home care, often from the first day it is needed. It will cover the cost for a visiting or live-in caregiver, companion, housekeeper, therapist or private duty nurse up to seven days a week, 24 hours a day (up to the policy benefit maximum). Other benefits of long-term care insurance include:

- Many individuals may feel uncomfortable relying on their children or family members for support. LTCI can help cover out-of-pocket expenses. Without this type of coverage, the cost of providing these services may quickly deplete the savings of the individual and/or their family.
- Premiums paid on a LTCI product may be eligible for an income tax deduction. The amount of the deduction depends on the age of the covered person. Benefits paid from a LTCI policy are generally excluded from income.
- Business deductions of premiums are determined by the type of business. For corporations paying premiums for an employee, they are generally 100% deductible if not included in employee's taxable income.

You qualify for covered benefits with most LTCI plans when you need help with two or more of six activities of daily living (ALDs) or when you have a cognitive impairment.

Most policies have an elimination period or waiting period. This is the period of time that you pay for care before your benefits are paid. The elimination period for most LTCI policies can be from 20 to 120 days. Longer elimination periods can result in lower premiums. Some policies can require intended claimants to provide proof of 20 to 120 service days of paid care before any benefits will be paid. In some cases, the option may be available to select zero elimination days, when covered services are provided in the home in accordance with a physician's Plan of Care.

Medicaid provides some benefits for LTCI. As a welfare program, Medicaid provides medically necessary services for people with limited resources who need nursing home care but can stay at home with special community care services. However, Medicaid generally does not cover LTC provided in a home setting or for assisted living.

Tax Advantages

There can be tax advantages associated with purchasing LTCI. As LTCI relates to personal income taxes there are two types of LTC policies which are offered.

- Tax Qualified (TQ): These policies are the most common policies offered. A TQ policy requires that a person meet either of two conditions. (1) they be expected to require care for at least 90 days and be **unable to perform 2 or more ADLs** such as eating, dressing, bathing, transferring, toileting, continence without substantial assistance (hands on or standby) or (2) for at least 90 days they need substantial assistance due to a severe cognitive impairment. In either case a physician must provide a Plan of Care. Benefits from a TQ policy are non-taxable.
- Non-tax Qualified (NTQ): These policies were formerly called traditional long term care insurance. The policy includes a trigger called a medical necessity trigger. What this means is

the patient's own physician, or a physician in conjunction with someone from the insurance company can state that the patient needs care for any medical reason and the policy will pay. NTQ policies include walking as an activity of daily living and usually only require the **inability to perform 1 or more ADLs**. The Treasury Department has not clarified the status of benefits received under a non-qualified LTCI plan. Therefore, the taxability of these benefits is open to further interpretation. This means that it is possible that individuals who receive benefits under a NTQ long-term care insurance policy risk facing a large tax bill for these benefits.

If your LTCI premiums are paid by yourself and are not part of a business expenses, there is a partial inclusion you can receive on your federal tax return if you itemize your deductions on Schedule A - Form 1040. You can include your premium payments, per limits below, as medical expenses on Schedule A. One of the IRS tax changes beginning in 2013 affects those under the age of 65. With your 2013 federal tax return you'll be able to deduct on Schedule A only the amount of your medical and dental expenses that is more than 10% of your adjusted gross income (AGI) from Form 1040, line 38. This increases from the 7.5% in previous years. **However, there is a temporary exemption from Jan. 1, 2013 to Dec. 31, 2016 for individuals age 65 and older and their spouses. If you or your spouse is 65 years or older or turned 65 during the tax year you are allowed to deduct unreimbursed medical care expenses that**

exceed 7.5% of your adjusted gross income. The threshold remains at 7.5% of AGI for those taxpayers until Dec. 31, 2016.

If you elected to pay your LTCI premiums with tax-free distributions from a retirement plan made directly to the insurance provider and these distributions would otherwise have been included in income these premiums cannot be included as a medical expense on Schedule A.

A qualified long-term care insurance contract provides only coverage of qualified long-term care services. The contract must:

- Be guaranteed renewable.
- Not provide for a cash surrender value or other money that can be paid, assigned, pledged or borrowed.
- Provide that refunds, other than refunds on the death of the insured or complete surrender or cancellation of the contract, and dividends under the contract must be used only to reduce future premiums or increase future benefits.
- Generally not pay or reimburse expenses incurred for services or items that would be reimbursed under Medicare, except where Medicare is a secondary payer, or the contract makes per diem or other periodic payments without regard to expenses.

The amount of qualified long-term care premiums you can include on Schedule A is limited by IRS guidelines. For 2014 the following amounts can be included.

1. Qualified long-term care premiums up to the amounts shown below for attained age before the close of the taxable year:

   - Age 40 or under – $370
   - Age 41 to 50 – $700
   - Age 51 to 60 – $1,400
   - Age 61 to 70 – $3,720
   - Age 71 or over – $4,660

2. Unreimbursed expenses for qualified long-term care services.

The limit on premiums is for each person. For example, both the husband and spouse have qualified LTCI policies and are both aged 65. His annual premium is $5,000/year while that of his wife's policy is $4,000/year. Though their combined premiums are $9,000/year, the maximum they could include on Schedule A, for medical and dental expenses, for 2014, would be $7,440 ($3,720 x 2). For more information on medical, health care and LTC expense deductibility you can refer to the IRS Publication 502, *Medical and Dental Expenses (including the Health Coverage Tax Credit)*.

LTCI State's Partnership Program

The federal *Deficit Reduction Act of 2005* authorized states to establish a Long-Term Care Insurance Partnership Program. A Partnership Program brings together a state government, private insurance companies that sell long-term care insurance, and residents who want to buy long-term care partnership policies. The purpose for creating this program is intended to alleviate the financial burden on states' Medicaid programs by encouraging individuals to purchase private LTCI. Four states; California, Connecticut, Indiana, and New York established partnership programs as part of a pilot project that began in 1987. However, the passage of the *Omnibus Budget Reconciliation Act (OBRA) of 1993* prohibited the program's expansion into other states. Today, all but 10 states have a Partnership LTCI Program. Except for California, these plans are also reciprocal among participating states. States must certify that partnership policies meet the specific requirements for their partnership program, including those who sell partnership policies are trained and understand how these policies relate to public and private coverage options.

A Partnership-qualified policy allows you to apply for Medicaid under modified eligibility rules that include a special feature called an asset disregard. These programs provide lifetime asset protection from the Medicaid spend-down requirement. What this means is that in return for purchasing partnership policies, a portion of the policyholders' assets will be disregarded when determining their eligibility for Medicaid LTC services, if and when they apply for such services. When applying for Medicaid LTC benefits, the partnership program allows individuals who purchase qualifying insurance policies to retain one dollar in assets for each dollar of long-term care insurance benefits paid by the policy. For example, the typical asset limit for an individual applying for Medicaid nursing home services is $2,000. If an applicant received $100,000 in benefits through a partnership program insurance policy, they may retain up to $102,000 of their assets when applying for Medicaid.

Qualifying LTCI policies must meet certain minimum requirements. Policies must be federally tax-qualified, provide inflation protection for policyholders of certain ages and only provide coverage to residents of the state where the policy coverage was offered. Often the only difference between a partnership-qualified policy and other long-term care insurance policies is the amount and type of inflation protection that the state requires.

LIFE INSURANCE AND LTC

If you don't have a LTCI policy there might be alternatives for paying the costs for LTC. Many life insurance products can pay a benefit through a policy rider to help cover LTC expenses. This living benefit enhances the value of life insurance to those seeking more than just a death benefit. Others allow you to sell your policy under certain circumstances. You'll need to review the language of your specific life insurance contract or call the insurance company who you have the policy with. You may be able to use your life insurance policy to help pay for long-term care services through the following options:

- Accelerated Death Benefits (ADB)
- Chronic Illness Rider
- Long-Term Care Rider
- Life settlements
- Viatical settlements

The first three bullet points cover these policy riders while the last two present situations allowing you to sell your life insurance policy to raise cash for LTC expenses. Some policy riders cover chronic illness situations, though some have broader coverage for long-term care services and can be marketed as long-term care insurance under many state regulations. Each rider opens accelerated access to a policy's death benefit while the insured is living. The qualification requirements for underwriting as well as for use and the benefits offered can differ significantly.

Accelerated Death Benefit

An accelerated death benefit (ADB) is a feature included in some life insurance policies that allows you to receive a tax-free advance on your life insurance death benefit while you are still alive. Sometimes the insurance company includes it in the policy for little or no cost. Other times the insurance company may require you to pay an extra premium to add this feature to your life insurance contract. There are different types of ADBs, each of which serves a different purpose. Depending on the type of policy you have, you may be able to receive a cash advance on your life insurance policy's death benefit if:

- You are terminally ill.
- You have a life-threatening diagnosis, such as AIDS.
- You need long-term care services for an extended amount of time.

- You are permanently confined to a nursing home and incapable of performing activities of daily living, such as bathing or dressing.

The amount of money you receive from these types of insurance policies varies, but typically the ADB payment amount is capped at 50 percent of the death benefit. The payments received from an ADB policy, while you are alive, are subtracted from the amount that will be paid to your beneficiaries when you die. However, there may be some policies out there which allow you to use the full amount of the death benefit.

For ADB policies that cover LTC services, the monthly benefit you can use for nursing home care is typically equal to two percent of the life insurance policy's face value. The amount available for home care (if it is included in the policy) is typically half that amount. For example, if your life insurance policy's face value is $200,000, then the monthly payout available to you for care in a nursing home would be $4,000, but only $2,000 for home care. Some policies may pay the same monthly amount for care regardless of where you receive the care.

Life Insurance with Chronic Illness Rider

An insurance rider, which is attached in a life insurance contract, refers to extra coverage or protection offered by the insurance contract aside from the primary coverage indicated in the policy. Since the rider is not originally covered in the policy, the insured might have to provide an additional payment for such rider. Some insurance policies may include this at no initial cost. However, administrative fees and expenses are usually triggered if the rider is activated by a chronic illness diagnosis. The cost may not be known until coverage is activated. This type of rider cannot be marketed as long-term care insurance and is usually an indemnity policy. The IRS enforces limits on the amount on income tax-free benefits that can be paid under the indemnity model. Any payments above this indemnity limit may be taxable to the insured. Currently, amounts paid over $320 per day or $116,800 per year may be taxable income unless receipts can be provided. If you have this rider, consult your tax specialist. The benefit is usually paid as a monthly, semi-annual or annual lump sum.

With a Chronic Illness Rider, a chronic illness is defined as a one-time permanent situation. It must be certified by a physician and the chronically ill individual must have a severe cognitive impairment or require substantial assistance with at least two activities of daily living **for the rest of their lifetime**. The benefit is usually available once in a lifetime. The Elimination Period may be 90 days or higher. Any remaining death benefit not accelerated through the rider will be paid as a death benefit.

Life Insurance with LTC Rider

The Long-Term Care Rider is usually a lower-cost method of providing some LTC insurance due to the fact that the insurer is simply paying out the life policy's proceeds before death, versus actually increasing the specified cash value amount of the policy. The rider could provide accelerated access up to 100% of the life insurance policy's specified amount if the insured suffers a qualified LTC event. With this rider there is usually an additional cost of insurance charge and expenses are based on the insured's age and their underwriting class. Costs are known at the time the policy is issued. Benefits under the LTC rider are income tax-free long term care payments under IRS code. Unlike the Chronic Illness Rider, **benefits for one or more LTC events are available throughout the insured's lifetime under the same LTC rider.**

Coverage becomes available when an insured is diagnosed with an illness or suffers an accident that requires substantial assistance with at least two ADLs for at least 90-days. The Elimination Period can depend on where LTC is received. Some policies may have 0 days for home care and 90 days for facility care. When looking at these LTC riders, as an alternative to "stand-alone" LTCI, make sure you completely review the features, benefits and premiums which are offered. This includes whether the rider pays in a reimbursement or first dollar basis, whether it pays the insured directly, as most do, or actually pays only to the facility providing care. A LTC rider normally allows the policyholder to utilize some or all of the policy's specified amount, or death benefit, for long term care costs, either for a period of time or until the available coverage amount has been exhausted, under stated terms; usually 2% or 3% of the specified amount per month. Make sure you are clear on how much the rider will pay and how, to whom and when. Premiums are often not the critical issue.

It's essential to make certain you understand that any pay-outs made for LTC under the LTC rider are deducted from the specified amount (and sometimes the cash-value amount as well) of the life insurance policy. At death the amount paid to your beneficiaries will be reduced, typically dollar for dollar, by the amount of LTC disbursements.

Life Settlement

Many individuals in their 60s, 70s and 80s were whipsawed by the Great Financial Recession of 2008-2009. More than one out of eight Americans, aged 40-60, is both raising children and caring for a parent. A life settlement may be a creative income generating option for some individuals. The Life Insurance Settlement Association, the national trade association, lists common reasons seniors sell their life insurance policies:

- A change in estate planning needs.
- The life insurance policy is no longer needed or wanted.
- Premium payments have become unaffordable.
- Changes in financial and life circumstances such as divorce, financial hardship or death of a beneficiary.
- The policy is about to lapse or surrender.

Life settlements allow you to sell your life insurance policy an agreed upon value to raise cash for any reason. There are no restrictions on how you chose to use the money. You may choose to use the proceeds to pay down loans or other outstanding debts, pay for essential expenses during your retirement or pay for long-term care services. A life settlement is usually only available to women age 74 and older and to men age 70 and older. The process can be very time consuming. There are items you should think about before you go this route. If you sell your life insurance policy, there may be little or no death benefit left for your heirs when you die. This could eliminate any legacy plans which you might have.

The Conning Research & Consulting 2011 study on life settlements found the average life settlement is 20% of the policy face value. Settlement offers can vary substantially depending on a policyholder's life expectancy and the premium costs. A shorter life expectancy means the provider pays the policy seller's premiums during a shorter period of time. The fewer costs associated with holding an active policy by the life settlement provider, the more cash a provider can return to the policyholder. The Conning 2011 study also found the average cash surrender value is only 10% of a policy's face value. In another study conducted in 2010, by the U.S. Government and Accountability Office, revealed consumers who sold their policies in a life settlement received an average of 700% more than if that same consumer had sold the policy back to the insurer for the policy's cash surrender value.

Once you find a life settlement provider you'll need to complete an application. The timeframe this entire process can take could be between 10-15 weeks, so this is NOT a quick way to receive cash proceeds. During this process the provider will collect medical information and obtain a copy of the life insurance policy. Once all the necessary documents are received, the provider will determine a settlement value and make an offer to the policyholder. If the policyholder accepts the offer, documents are prepared to transfer ownership of the policy. Once document are signed, the funding organization will submits these and requests a change of policy ownership. In the final step the ownership and beneficiary changes are verified and recorded and settlement funds are wire transferred into the account designated by the policyholder.

There may be tax consequences as proceeds may be taxed. The IRS can consider some or all funds from a life settlement as taxable. The amount recouped up to the cumulative premiums, which have been paid by the policyholder, are usually tax-free. Additional monies received up to the cash surrender value can be treated as ordinary income. Any excess cash above the cash surrender value could be considered a capital gain. Considering all the taxes which could be paid on a life settlement, the costs could outweigh the benefit. If you're considering a life settlement you should definitely consult with a tax expert.

Life settlements are labor-intensive during which the policyholder must be evaluated and submit medical records. Even after the transaction is complete, the policy seller must provide regular health updates. How does the life settlement provider get paid? After the policyholder receives his life settlement, the provider finances the premium payments until the policy seller dies, then redeems the insurance contract for its full face value.

Many individuals will eventually need to rely upon Medicaid coverage for their long-term care services in a nursing home. In a twist in Medicaid planning, several states, including Florida, Kentucky and Texas have proposed legislation which would allow the consumer to use a life settlement to help fund long-term care. These assets would not count in determining Medicaid eligibility whereas in their life insurance form they would. The proceeds from the life settlement would be held in an irrevocable state or federally insured account with a schedule of payments to provide for LTC. All of these proposals include a provision that any amounts remaining in the individual's account with the state be refunded as a death benefit if they are not needed to cover LTC costs. This would be an alternative to surrender the life insurance policy which could provide the policyholder with a greater cash benefit. For now, Florida's proposal *HB 535-Medicaid Eligibility* died in the Health Innovation Subcommittee in May 2013.

Viatical Settlement

A viatical settlement allows you to sell your life insurance policy to a third party and use the money you receive to pay for care. Most viatical settlement companies pay a lump sum typically up to 75% of the face value of your policy, depending on your life expectancy and the expected policy premiums for the remainder of the life of the insured.

The viatical settlement industry got started in the 1990's. In the early days you could have gotten a higher percentage in your settlement. However, as of 2010, several factors have changed the rules of the game. Adjustments to Life Expectancy Tables, medical advances, and industry trends have all resulted in a lowering of the payoff values for policies. The benefit you receive is based on your life expectancy.

Somewhat like ADBs, a viatical settlement is only possible if you are terminally ill. Viatical settlements can be done by someone of any age who has been diagnosed with a life-threatening illness and is expected to die within twenty-four months. Since one of the key variables in pricing the deal is estimating how long you've got left, do **not** rely on life expectancy estimates provided by viatical medical underwriting companies without first speaking with your own physician. If you accept the terms of the offer, the viatical company becomes the owner of your policy and is its beneficiary. The viatical company also takes over payment of premiums on the policy. As a result, you get money to pay for LTC costs and the viatical company receives the full death benefit after you die.

Table 10.2 Viatical Benefits Received Based on Life Expectancy

Life Expectancy	Benefit (%)
1 – 6 months	80
6 – 12 months	70
12 – 18 months	65
18 – 24 months	60
Over 24 months	50

Courtesy: National Clearinghouse for Long Term Care Information

The National Association of Insurance Commissioners (NAIC) provides guidelines as to how that percent should vary based on your remaining life expectancy as illustrated in table 10.2 on the previous page..

Don't accept partial payment or installment payments from a viatical provider, and insist that all the money be placed in an escrow account until the transaction is completed. Your heirs will not receive a death benefit if you use the viatical settlement option.

The proceeds received from a properly executed viatical settlement is tax-free, if you have a life expectancy of two years or less or are chronically ill, and the viatical company is licensed in the state in which it does business. You should know that viatical companies approve less than 50% of applicants. Viatical settlements are complicated contracts with both legal and financial elements.

Final Thoughts Concerning LTCI

The final decision as to whether or not to buy LTCI comes down to 2 main issues, which are not equally weighted. The first is your mental disposition. The first wave of the Baby Boom generation turned 65 in 2011. There will be 78,000,000 turning 65 over the next 17 years. I am in this generation, though later in time. This was a generation who once believed; never trust anyone over 30. A generation who loved its music and never thought they would get old. That was then and this is now. Like other risks you need to decide if you have the ability to "self-insure" if the time comes. Sudden, unexpected events can have a long lasting impact. Where will the financial assistance come from to pay for this ongoing care?

The second decision is based on income levels and cash flow needs. If you have the financial assets and resources, you should at least consider insuring some of the LTC risk. The three most important reasons why not to wait are:

1. The longer you wait, the greater the chance you have of becoming uninsurable due to a medical event or chronic illness. Your eligibility is based

on your current physical health and mental acuity at the time of your application submission.

2. Your LTCI premiums are based on your age at the time you submit your application. The longer you wait the more it will cost when you apply.

Once you're approved, your premium rate does not increase as you age or if your health deteriorates. The insurance company can increase premiums on an entire class basis but not on just your policy.

2013 – THE CURRENT ENVIRONMENT

Over the last ten years the number of carriers who provide LTCI has dropped from over a hundred companies to about two dozen key players. In 2009, Allianz Life Insurance Company of North America got out. In 2010, MetLife exited the business. In 2011, Guardian Life Insurance Company of America stopped offering the policies. In 2012, Unum Group dropped out of the group LTC business and Prudential Financial Inc. stopped offering individual LTC insurance but continued to provide coverage for employer-based groups. According to Moody's Investor Service, in 2012 Genworth and John Hancock (a subsidiary of Manulife Financial Corporation) represented 23% and 16% of the LTCI market share, respectively. Aegon NV's Transamerica unit, Bankers Life and Casualty, Northwestern Mutual Life Insurance Company and Mutual of Omaha Insurance Company are the other major players in the market today.

What's causing this seismic shift in the business? Three major forces are currently squeezing the LTC business.

- Increases in life expectancies of the individuals buying the coverage.
- Underpricing of premiums on in-force policies.
- Low returns on the fixed-income portfolios that pay claims.

Many insurance companies made miscalculations or used overly optimistic assumptions about these issues and offered policies at lower prices, expecting to make money by paying fewer claims and getting higher returns on their investment portfolios. In addition, the lapse rate on issued policies has been falling. The lapse rate is, the number of policyholders, who stop paying their premiums and let their policies expire. Underwriters anticipated 5% to 6% of policyholder's would let their plans lapse. Actually experience has been closer to 1% to 2%, according to insurance commissioner for the state of Nevada. Together these factors are creating a block of business which is building sizable liabilities for the LTCI insurers.

The Federal Reserve has pumped trillions of reserves into the banking system to keep short-term interest rates low to support the fledgling economy and repair the banking system. Low inflation, a desire for safety plus massive bond purchases by the Fed have resulted in long-term interest rates falling also. The current interest rate environment is creating havoc within the insurance industry. According to the *American Association for Long-Term Care Insurance (AALTCI)* 40%-60% of the money insurers accumulate to cover future claims comes from the investment returns of their portfolios. Insurance portfolio managers are now seeking higher returns by increasing their credit risk exposure and/or lengthening the duration of their holdings by assuming increased interest rate risk.

With LTC increasing at an average of 4.7% to 6.6% a year, LTC insurance providers have now begun changing their assumptions. According to the AALTCI this is leading to higher costs for new LTC policies. New policies are 17% higher in price that they were one year ago. Besides premium increases, another major change that's already occurring is gender-distinct pricing. Genworth was the first to introduce this in April 2013, followed later by Transamerica, John Hancock and Mutual of Omaha. Studies show women are two to three times more likely than men to require LTC and, on average, require that care for a longer period. Women accounted for 66% of the $6.6 billion in LTCI claim benefits paid out in 2012. Unisex pricing is still available in 25 states, including California, Florida and New York though it's just a matter of time before more states adopt this trend. According to the AALTCI, earlier this year these insurers introduced new policies which charged single women an average of 40% and 60% more than a comparably aged single man.

In its January 2014 release of its *2014 National Long-Term Care Insurance Price Index*, the AALTCI indicated that a 55-year old, single male purchasing new LTCI protection can expect to pay $925 per year for $164,000 of benefits. He'll pay $1,765 for coverage which increases the benefit pool to $365,000 at age 85, a 14.5% decline from the previous year's average. A 55-

year old, single female, would pay an average of $1,225 per year for the same level of $164,000 in benefits. The typical woman will pay an average of 12% more than in 2013. For a couple where both spouses are age 60, purchasing $164,000 of immediate coverage will cost about $2,000 per year. For the same age couple purchasing $164,000 of immediate coverage which grows to a combined benefit pool of $730,000 ($365,000 each) at age 85 is about $3,840 in premium costs per year. The range of coverage cost was as wide as $2,700 to $5,400 per year. According to the National Association of Insurance Commissioners (NAIC), a 50-year old buying a new policy will pay an average of $888 a year; a 65-year old average of $1,850 and a 75-year old, $5,880. The NAIC also recommends that consumers should typically spend no more than 7% of their income on long-term care insurance.

Many companies are becoming less willing to insure individuals with health issues. Some of the most popular policy features such as lifetime benefit period and limited pay are no longer available in some policies. In addition, carriers are re-evaluating the inflation protection feature of these policies. It was very common in older policies to have a 5% compounded inflation rider. How can the insurance company increase your benefit at 5% when long-term U.S. Government bond yield about 3.5%. This is what has been responsible for much of the premium increases. Look at a simple inflation rate as opposed to a compound rate. Consumers need to be creative when look for LTC coverage.

The real problem is the business which has been written over the course of the last two decades. To raise premiums on existing policies the LTCI providers must file requests with state insurance regulators. Many LTCI providers are now raising prices on existing in-force business. The rate hikes in LTC premiums over the past few years have been staggering. Earlier in 2013, Genworth indicated it had requested premium increases of up to 95% on some of its individual LTC products. John Hancock recently indicated they would file requests with state insurance regulators to raise premiums on 50% of its in-force business by an average of 25%. This comes three years after the insurer asked state regulators for rate hikes averaging 40%. Genworth Financial started filing for rate increases of 6% to 13% on its in-force business which was purchased between 2003 and 2012.

Before the last 3-5 years, LTC insurance had been priced much like life insurance policies, where premiums remained the same over time. With the massive rate increases which have been see in premiums and those requested by LTCI carriers over the last 3-5 years, we may begin to see premiums stabilize in a sense. LTCI may begin to be priced more like traditional health insurance going forward where periodic rate increases of 2% to 4% may be seen. If premiums rise by too much it could cause healthy policyholders to drop their coverage due to cost, thus creating a larger pool of policyholders who most likely will need LTC.

Will you really need LTC? No one knows for certain but specific factors may increase your odds of some medical event occurring. The older you get the more likely you'll need some sort of assistance. If you live alone, you're more likely to need paid care as opposed to if you're married. Women are more likely to need LTC, simply because women tend to live longer than men. A chronically poor diet along with bad exercise habits will increase your chances. Your family medical history may give clues as to past conditions among family members or relatives. The industry is totally different than it was twenty years ago and LTC facilities are different also.

FINAL THOUGHT

Let's look at the following situation. Your father passed away a number of years ago. Your mother's health subsequently deteriorated and she's now been in a nursing home for a few years. Her cost of care has been rising steadily over the years and she has limited financial resources. You realize her expenses are now exceeding her ability to pay and begin to look into Medicaid as an alternative. Can you, as the adult child, be held fiscally responsible for your mother's nursing bills?

Believe it or not the answer is yes! Even if you have other siblings, you _could_ be singled out and held fiscally responsible for your parent's nursing home and other LTC expenses. There is a law which is on the books' in about 30 states and can vary somewhat from state to state. These laws are known as _filial support laws_. The law generally provides that a spouse, child and/or parent have the responsibility to maintain or financially assist an indigent person. These are two exceptions in the law. The first is if an individual doesn't have sufficient financial ability to support the indigent person. The second would be the case where a child would not be liable for the support of a parent who abandoned the child when he or she was a minor for a specific period of time. While these laws have been on states' books for decades, they were rarely enforced until recently. The *Deficit Reduction Act of 2005*, signed by President Bush, made it more difficult for individuals to transfer assets before qualifying for Medicaid coverage of nursing home costs. Filial laws are being enforced more frequently to make children of LTC recipients responsible for their parents' LTC costs.

This was recently highlighted in a 2012 Pennsylvania case, *Health Care & Retirement Corporation of America v. Pittas*, which received national attention. The case went to an appeals court where it ruled that John Pittas, 47, was liable for his mother's $93,000 nursing home bill under Pennsylvania's filial laws. This was despite the fact that the mother had applied to Medicaid to cover her cost of care, the son had done nothing wrong and there were three other potentially responsible individuals; the mother's husband and two other adult children. The law does not make all family members responsible, let alone equally.

This case highlights the fact that many companies in the nursing home care business, when given a choice, might prefer private pay over Medicaid reimbursed expenses. The nursing home company can pick and choose who they sue without regard for family discord which will likely ensue. With chronic federal government deficits and a Medicaid program whose costs are going to explode in some states due to the implementation of the ACA, a rise in filial law cases may be just on the horizon.

If you are reasonable well off financially, you need to check your state laws and if you have aged parents, include them in your own planning process for LTC. If you're going to purchase a LTCI product, take the time to read the fine print. You may be purchasing the policy but somewhere down the road it may be your adult-child filing the claim. If you don't include them in your planning process they may not be familiar with the intent of your original plan.

"General revenue - what taxpayers are willing to give government, what they think is fair to give government - is not going to grow at the same amount that the federal government basically forces us to spend on Medicaid."

Rick Scott
Republican
45th Governor - Florida
Businessman

CHAPTER ELEVEN

THE MEDICAID PROGRAM

Medicaid was created by the *Social Security Amendments of 1965*, which added Title XIX to the *Social Security Act*. As with Medicare, the Medicaid program has changed through the years. In 1990, under the *Omnibus Budget Reconciliations Act (OBRA-90)*, the *Medicaid Drug Rebate* and the *Health Insurance Premium Payment* programs were created. The *OBRA-93* brought changes to the Medicaid Drug Rebate Program as well as requiring states to implement a Medicaid estate recovery program to sue the estates of decedents for medical care costs paid by Medicaid. Medicaid is a welfare program to provide benefits for the indigent and impoverished which means people and families with low incomes and resources. The *Balanced Budget Act of 1997* added the Children's Health Insurance Program (CHIP). Then in

2010, the *Patient Protection and Affordability Care Act (PPACA)* expanded eligibility starting in 2014. Individuals with incomes up to 138% of the poverty line will qualify for coverage including adults without dependent children.

Medicaid is separate from Medicare. Medicaid is a joint federal-state program. Each state administers its own Medicaid program which must conform to federal guidelines in order for the state to receive matching funds and grants. The CMS monitors the state-run programs and establishes requirements for service delivery, quality, funding and eligibility standards. Medicaid provides health coverage to the following:

- 31 million children, including half of all low-income children.
- 11 million, non-disabled adults.
- 8.8 million, individuals with disabilities.
- 4.6 million, low-income seniors, nearly all of whom are enrolled in Medicare. Also covers 3.7 million individuals with disabilities who are enrolled in Medicare.

In total, 8.3 million people are "dual eligible" and enrolled in both Medicaid and Medicare composing more than 17% of all Medicaid enrollees. Medicaid payments currently assist nearly 60% of all nursing home residents. It also provides financing for 40% of all childbirths in the U.S. Since each state administers its own Medicaid program a broad overview of the Medicaid program and its benefits is presented.

AFFORDABLE CARE ACT

The Affordable Care Act (ACA) fills in current gaps in coverage for the poorest Americans by creating a minimum Medicaid income eligibility level across the country. Beginning in January 2014, individuals under 65 years of age with income below 133% of the federal poverty level (FPL) will be eligible for Medicaid. In 2013 this is about $21,404 for a family of two or $32,499 for a family of four. Eligible individuals may enroll in Medicaid or CHIP at any time during the year. For the first time, low-income adults without children will be guaranteed coverage through Medicaid in every state without need for a waiver, and parents of children will be eligible at a uniform income level across all states. Medicaid and Children's Health Insurance Program (CHIP) eligibility and enrollment will be much simpler and will be coordinated with the newly created Health Insurance Marketplace. The Medicaid and CHIP programs provide free or low-cost health insurance coverage. Medicaid is administered by each state to provide health care coverage to low-income individuals, families and children and also the elderly and individuals with disabilities.

The federal government currently pays about 57% of the cost of current Medicaid enrollees in each state. The authors of the ACA realized the federal government would need to provide an incentive for the state's to participate in what would likely be a significantly increase in "newly eligible" participants. Coverage for these newly eligible adults will be fully funded by the federal government at 100% for 2014, 2015 and 2016. It will then be phased down to 95% in

2017, 94% in 2018, 93% in 2019 and 90% in 2020 and all subsequent years.

Beginning in 2014, individuals with incomes of $15,000 or less will qualify for Medicaid in about half of all the states. The program is designed to be very affordable for every participant and cost-sharing is extremely limited. Every state's Medicaid and CHIP program is changing and improving. To easily see each state clink this link, www.medicaid.gov/Medicaid-CHIP-Program-information/By-State/By-State.html.

When individuals apply for health coverage through the Marketplace they are automatically screened for Medicaid eligibility. Depending on the state, the Marketplace will either assess or determine individuals' eligibility for Medicaid coverage. If individuals are assessed as eligible, they will be informed that their application will be sent to the state Medicaid agency for a final eligibility determination. If individuals are determined eligible for Medicaid, the Marketplace will notify consumers directly and the individual will then be given the option to enroll in a Medicaid plan.

The ACA also creates a new office within CMS, the Medicare-Medicaid Coordination Office, to coordinate care for individuals who are dual-eligible for both Medicaid and Medicare.

ELIGIBILITY

According to the CMS, in 2001 46 million Americans received their health care coverage through the Medicaid program. By 2010, nearly 60 million Americans receive health care coverage through Medicaid and CHIP. The rules for Medicaid eligibility are different for each state. To determine if you qualify you can use the link, www.healthcare.gov/do-i-qualify-for-medicaid/. Once there you can get your specific state information by selecting your state in the drop-down menu at the bottom of the page.

In order to participate in Medicaid, federal law requires states to cover certain population groups which are considered mandatory eligibility groups and gives the states the flexibility to cover other population groups which are called optional eligibility groups. For many eligibility groups, income is calculated in relation to a percentage of the Federal Poverty Level (FPL) which is updated annually. Poverty guidelines for 2013 for the 48 contiguous states and the District of Columbia are:

Table 11.1 Annual FPL Guidelines for 2014 for the 48 Contiguous States and Washington D.C.

Percent of Poverty Guidelines (in dollars rounded up)								
Family Size	1	2	3	4	5	6	7	8
100%	11,670	15,730	19,790	23,850	27,910	31,970	36,030	40,090
120%	14.004	18,876	23,748	28,620	33,492	38,364	43,236	48,108
133%	15,521	20,921	26,321	31,721	37,121	42,521	47,920	53,320
135%	15,755	21,236	26,717	32,198	37,679	43,160	48,641	54,122
150%	17,505	23,595	29,685	35,775	41,865	47,955	54,045	60,135
175%	20,423	27,528	34,633	41,738	48,843	55,948	63,053	70,158
185%	21,590	29,101	36,612	44,123	51,634	59,145	66,656	74,167
200%	23,340	31,460	39,580	47,700	55,820	63,940	72,060	80,180
250%	29,175	39,325	49,475	59,625	69,775	79,925	90,075	100,225

Source: Medicaid

For family units of more than 8 members, add $4,060 for each additional member. Poverty guidelines for Alaska and Hawaii have higher income thresholds. For other groups income standards are based on income or other non-financial criteria standards for other programs, such as the Supplemental Security Income (SSI) program.

Within each category there are requirements other than income that must be met. These other requirements include, but are not limited to, assets, age, pregnancy, disability, blindness, income and resources and one's status as a U.S. citizen or a lawfully admitted immigrant.

QUALIFICATIONS

To qualify for Medicaid, consumers must also meet certain financial requirements. Under the ACA the formula for determining Medicaid eligibility will be streamlined and unified across states. The formula is based on modified adjusted gross income (MAGI). MAGI is a methodology for how income is counted and how household composition and family size are determined. Beginning October 1, 2013, MAGI must be used in most eligibility determinations for children and non-disabled adults under age 65, whether or not a state chooses to expand adult Medicaid coverage. MAGI is based on federal tax rules for determining adjusted gross income which include:

- Earned income (e.g., wages, salary, or any compensation for work).
- Self-employment income from a business or hobby.

- Social Security income, including Social Security Disability Insurance (SSDI) and retirement benefits.
- Unemployment benefits.
- Investment income, including interest, dividends, and capital gains.

Family size will now be defined using the tax filing definition. It will include those dependents that are reported and included when a family submits its federal income tax return. Applicants who do not file federal income tax returns and aren't claimed as dependents on someone else's federal tax return can base their household size on the immediate family members who live together.

There are some types of income that count under non-MAGI rules which aren't counted for MAGI determinations. This includes child support and veterans' benefits.

BENEFITS

Each state determines the type, amount, duration and scope of services they will provide within broad federal guidelines. However, some benefits which each state is required to cover are mandatory benefits while some states can choose to provide optional benefits through the Medicaid program. Medicaid does not pay benefits to individuals directly but sends benefit payments directly to the health care providers. Mandatory benefits include the following:

- Inpatient hospital services
- Outpatient hospital services

- Early and Periodic Screening, Diagnostic, and Treatment (EPSDT) services
- Nursing facility services
- Home health services
- Physician services
- Rural health clinic services
- Federally qualified health center services
- Laboratory and X-ray services
- Family planning services
- Nurse Midwife services
- Certified Pediatric and Family Nurse Practitioner services
- Freestanding Birth Center services (when licensed or otherwise recognized by the state)
- Transportation to medical care
- Tobacco cessation counseling for pregnant women
- Tobacco Cessation

Optional benefits covered by each state could include:

- Prescription drugs
- Clinic services
- Physical therapy
- Occupational therapy
- Speech, hearing and language disorder services
- Respiratory care services
- Other diagnostic, screening, preventive and rehabilitative services
- Podiatry services
- Optometry services
- Dental services
- Dentures
- Prosthetics

- Eyoglasses
- Chiropractic services
- Other practitioner services
- Private duty nursing services
- Personal Care
- Hospice
- Case management
- Services for Individuals Age 65 or Older in an Institution for Mental Disease (IMD)
- Services in an intermediate care facility for the mentally retarded
- State Plan Home and Community Based Services
- Self-Directed Personal Assistance Services
- Community First Choice Option
- TB Related Services
- Inpatient psychiatric services for individuals under age 21
- Other services approved by the Secretary*

LOOK-BACK PROVISIONS

There was a time when financial planners engaged in Medicaid planning. The goal was to help middle-class clients become *artificially* impoverished by transferring assets so they became eligible for Medicaid. It is currently a misdemeanor for advisors/agents to assist clients in participating in Medicaid planning. To prevent this abuse in the program, Medicaid implemented a look-back period for assets that might have been transferred at less than fair value. The *Deficit Reduction Act of 2005 (DRA)* significantly changed the rules governing the treatment of asset transfers and homes of nursing

221

home residents. The look-back period was changed from 3 years to 5 years. States are required to apply the DRA to their state programs because Medicaid is run by both the state and federal government.

INELIGIBILITY PERIOD

Asset transfers during the look-back period trigger the ineligibility period. The length of the ineligibility period is calculated by dividing the amount transferred by the average monthly cost of nursing home care in your area. The penalty period or ineligibility period for transferred assets is the date when the person applies for Medicaid - generally when the person enters a nursing home. That means that any transfers without fair market value (gifts of any kind) made by the Medicaid applicant during the preceding five years are penalized, dollar for dollar. All transfers made during the five-year look-back period are totaled, and the applicant is penalized that amount.

An example will help to put this in context. After Ted's death, Elizabeth gave her vacation home to her daughter Kimberly. The market value of the home was $200,000 and the monthly cost of nursing home care was $5,000 in Elizabeth's region. Elizabeth's ineligibility period is therefore 40 months ($200,000/$5,000 per month = 40 months). The ineligibility period begins to run when Elizabeth applies for Medicaid and seeks long-term care assistance and expires 40 months from that date. However, if she gives the house to Kimberly **more than five years before her application date**, the look-back period would have expired no penalty period would be imposed.

Before the *DRA*, the ineligibility period would have started on the date that Elizabeth gave the vacation home to Kimberly. Now, the ineligibility period begins when Elizabeth applies for Medicaid, which is later than when she gave the home to Kimberly.

PRIVATIZING MEDICAID – THE FUTURE

In June 2013, federal officials gave final approval to Florida's Medicaid managed care program, essentially privatizing parts of Florida's Medicaid program. The state's Medicaid costs have been rising annually. For 2013-2014, Medicaid expenditures are projected to rise above $22 billion. Through this program Florida will move nearly 3 million Medicaid recipients from Medicaid's normal fee-for-service care into private HMOs by the beginning of 2014.

Florida's legislature first passed the initiative in 2011; then spent the next two years negotiating with Federal officials. As a result of those negotiations Florida also agreed to several regulations and consumer safeguards including:

- A rapid-cycle system for recipient complaints.
- Increased recipient participation in Florida Medical Care Advisory Committee.
- Continuation of current services for up to 60 days after enrollment.
- HMO validation by Florida's External Quality Assurance Organization.

It's expected this new program will help to curb future cost increases while improving the quality of care.

The most costly Medicaid patients to care for are those that are receiving long-term care benefits. The transition to the new program is going to begin with roughly 90,000 long-term care patients on Medicaid. They will have the choice of enrolling in one of seven available state-approved HMOs. Many have already enrolled and those that have not yet will have until December 1, 2013 to choose a plan. Under this program Medicaid funds will first be paid out to these select insurance carriers. Funds will be used to pay nursing homes, in-home caregivers and other elder care providers.

Florida is the first state to take this approach in hopes of creating greater efficiencies leading to cost savings. Nationwide, Medicaid payments assist nearly 60% of all nursing home residents. The retirement age population is growing larger every day. States will need to get creative in how they deal with the growing number of elderly who will probably qualify for Medicaid and ultimately need LTC.

One option is introducing legislation which would allow seniors to sell their life insurance policies; then designate the use of the proceeds to augment their LTC expenses. Texas has already passed similar legislation to allow seniors this option. Their new law allows seniors to use the proceeds from their policies to pay for the LTC providers of their choosing. Florida introduced a bill earlier in 2013 but the bill did not get out of the sub-committee.

CONTACT YOUR RESIDENT STATE FOR MORE INFORMATION

State participation in Medicaid is voluntary. However, all states have participated since 1982 when Arizona formed its Arizona Health Care Cost Containment System (AHCCCS) program. Medicaid and CHIP program information varies by state. Go to www.medicaid.gov; then choose your state profile. In some states Medicaid is subcontracted to private health insurance companies while other states pay health care providers such as physicians, clinics and hospitals directly. Many attorneys now specialized in Medicaid planning. If you hire an attorney these are some fundamental questions to ask.

- How does our state define assets? Are any of the transfers of property "exempt"?
- How do transfers of property between spouses affect eligibility?
- What's the maximum amount of assets a person can retain in my state and still qualify for Medicaid?

"But here's what I would tell people of my generation. I turn 40 this year. There isn't going to be Social Security. There isn't going to be a Medicare when you retire. Forget about what your benefit is going to look like. There isn't going to be one if we don't make some reforms to save that program now."

Marco Rubio
Republican U.S. Senator – Florida
Speaker of the Florida House of Representatives
Florida House of Representatives – 11th District
Lawyer and City Commissioner

CHAPTER TWELVE

WHAT YOU NEED TO KNOW BEFORE YOU BUY

At this juncture, let's do a quick recap of what's been covered. Eligibility and enrollment periods have been explained as well as disenrollment. All the different programs have been covered in detail, including original Medicare Part A and Part B, Medicare Advantage Part C plans, Medicare Prescription Drug Part D plans and Medicare Supplement/Medigap plans along with long-term care and Medicaid. Now the decision making process is up to you. You have to decide what to get and who you want to work with.

Your first decision is what coverage you think is most appropriate for you, given your health status and income levels. If you just want only original Medicare Part A and Part B you will need to enroll yourself through Social Security. Refer back to Chapter 4. Online is probably the quickest and easiest method.

Your second decision will be if you want more coverage than what original Medicare provides. If you want to add a Medicare Supplement/Medigap plan, enroll in a Medicare Advantage plan or enroll in a Medicare Prescription Drug plan, you will need to purchase those plans through a private insurance company which has been approved by and contracted with Medicare. Then you need to decide which plan is best for you and who do you buy it from?

You have two options. One is to deal directly with the insurance company and its licensed insurance agents ("agents"). They are employees of the insurance company. The other is to work with an independent licensed insurance agent. These insurance agents usually work in one of two ways. (1) They can be contracted and appointed, as an independent agent, with only one insurance company. They may do this only part time, such as during the Annual Enrollment Period each year which lasts 8 weeks between October and December. The agent may feel an affinity for working with only one insurance company. The insurance company pays them a fixed commission based on the type of plan they sell. (2) They may be an independent insurance agent working for themselves and contracted and appointed with a number of different insurance companies. Each insurance company pays the agent a commission directly based on the type of plan they sell. These agents are then able to offer their clients choices and different options when accessing their needs.

It's important to note there is NO DIFFERENCE between a plan purchased directly from an insurance company or purchased through an independent agent working with that insurance company.

This brings us to the third decision you have to make. Who do you buy from? There's nothing wrong if you want to be a complete do-it-yourselfer in the creation, implementation and management of your personal Medicare strategy as long as you are fully aware of the consequences of the decisions you make and will fully accept the responsibility for the outcomes that arise. You're good to go. The buck stops with you. You will need to do all your own research, either by contacting a variety of different insurance companies directly or by going online. Then you need to compare all the plans you've researched to decide what's best for you.

If you have an affinity for a particular branded insurance company, working with the agent of that company may be best for you. Remember, since they only represent one company and their products they clearly have a bias in getting you to buy their plan. If you decide to work with an independent agent make sure they represent at least 3-4 insurance companies. That way when you sit down with them to review the benefits, features and cost of the plans you have some choice in comparing which plan might be best for you. However, if you choose to engage the services of an independent licensed insurance agent that individual may represent themselves as a financial planner, investment advisor, stock broker, money manager or insurance agent. Remember you are bringing a degree of trust into the relationship and that individual needs to fully respect that and continue to earn it.

With the flood of baby boomers turning 65 and entering the Medicare maze of health care options for the first time the industry is ripe for individuals to enter the business believing they can make enormous sums of money by pushing products that may or may not be suitable. As the late former President Ronald Regan once said, *"Trust, but verify."* The onus is on you to check out any Medicare Advantage, Medicare Prescription Drug or Medicare Supplement/Medigap plan you may be considering buying. **Don't be afraid to ask a lot of questions. It's your health and your money.**

In 2008, new rules were adopted by the federal Centers for Medicare and Medicaid Services (CMS). These rules were designed to crack down on predatory sales practices in the $51 billion Medicare Advantage industry. Some of these changes included a ban on cold-calling and restrictions on agent compensation. For example, in 2011 the agent bonus per enrollee for enrollment in a Medicare Advantage plan was $403, compared to an agent bonus of $53 for enrollment in a Medicare Prescription Part D Drug plan.

Figure 12.1 Agent Bonus

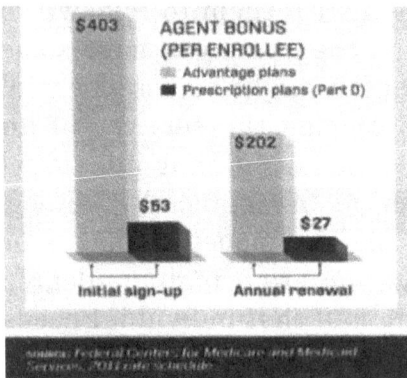

Some states have even higher compensation rates. Figure 12.1, to the left, illustrates this along with renewal bonuses which are paid each year for up to five years on renewal of the plan.

Courtesy: MONEY, December 2011

After the new rules were adopted, the CMS did see a drop of 45% in the number of complaints they received.

In a 2010 report done by the Office of Inspector General for the Department of Health and Human Services, 64% of complaints by enrollees were for getting misleading information.

Figure 12.2 Complaints
By Enrollee

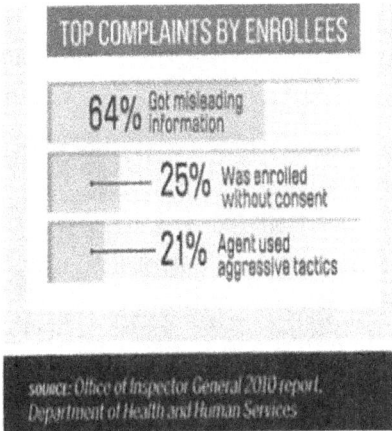

TOP COMPLAINTS BY ENROLLEES

64% Got misleading information

25% Was enrolled without consent

21% Agent used aggressive tactics

SOURCE: Office of Inspector General 2010 report. Department of Health and Human Services

Figure 12.2, to the left, illustrates that after that complaint, the next two most common complaints received were being enrolled without consent and an agent who used aggressive sales tactics to get them to buy from them.

Courtesy: MONEY, December 2011

Watch out for illegal sales practices. According to the CMS, it's illegal for anyone to do the following:

- Pressure you into buying a Medicare Supplement policy, or lie to or mislead you to switch from one company or policy to another.
- Sell you a second Medicare Supplement policy when they know that you already have one unless you tell the insurance company in writing that you plan to cancel your existing Medicare Supplement policy.
- Sell you a Medicare Supplement policy if they know you have Medicaid, except in certain situations.

231

- Sell you a Medicare Supplement policy if they know you're in a Medicare Advantage plan unless coverage under the Medicare Advantage plan will end before the effective date of the Medicare Supplement policy.
- Claim that a Medicare Supplement policy is part of the Medicare Program or any other federal program. Medicare Supplement insurance is private health insurance.
- Claim that a Medicare Advantage plan is a Medicare Supplement policy.
- Sell you a Medicare Supplement policy that can't be legally sold in your state. Check with your State Insurance Department to make sure that the Medicare Supplement policy you're interested in can be sold in your state.
- Misuse the names, letters or symbols of the U.S. Department of Health & Human Services (HHS), Social Security Administration (SSA), Centers for Medicare & Medicaid Services (CMS), or any of their various programs like Medicare. (For example, they can't suggest the Medicare Supplement policy has been approved or recommended by the federal government.)
- Claim to be a Medicare representative if they work for a Medicare Supplement insurance company.
- Sell you a Medicare Advantage Plan when you say you want to stay in original Medicare and buy a Medicare Supplement policy. A Medicare Advantage plan isn't the same as original Medicare. If you enroll in a Medicare Advantage plan you can't use a Medicare Supplement policy.

If you believe that a federal law has been broken, call the Inspector General's hotline at 1-800-HHS-TIPS (1-800-447-8477). TTY users should call 1-800-377-4950. Your State Health Insurance Department can help you with other insurance related problems.

What if you've already gotten into a Medicare Advantage plan you're not happy with? If you're into the next year you're going to have to wait until the next Annual Enrollment Period (AEP) to make a change. If you buy one plan during AEP and then decide it's not right for you, as long as you are still in AEP you can make a change into another plan. However, if you wait until the coming year, during the Disenrollment Period, you can only drop your Medicare Advantage plan and return to original Medicare. You can't switch from one Medicare Advantage plan to another.

The magazine MONEY had an article, *Beware of Medicare Hucksters*, in its December 2011 issue. It's an excellent read of what can go wrong. Several examples were cited involving individuals. Much of the article is focused on issues involving Medicare Advantage plans.

Health care options and choices are probably much more confusing to individuals than investment choices. It can lead to "choice overload". If you make a bad investment choice you see the results of that decision each day and can make necessary changes if you so choose. If you make a bad health care choice you may not know the consequences until well after the medical event has occurred, treatment has been rendered and you leave the hospital. When all the bills start coming in and you see what was not covered by your insurance policy; you then realize that your options are probably going to be very limited in what you can do. So what can you do?

Do your homework and plan ahead so you won't feel like you're being rushed into a decision when the Annual Enrollment Period begins during in fourth quarter. When you are looking at the plans benefits, features and costs, fully understanding the following key points should assist you in arriving at the best purchase decision.

- Always read the sales material and documents. Don't go by what the agent only says. They may not know all the coverage details.
- What are copay dollar amounts?
- What are the coinsurance percentages?
- What are the deductibles and if there are any caps?
- Do you understand what procedures are covered and what type of facilities can be used?
- Are your existing physicians (PCP and specialists) covered in the plan?
- Does the plan cover the hospitals you have procedures done at?
- Are your existing prescription drugs covered?
- Don't make a snap decision. The terms of the plan won't change in a week if you want to take time and think it over.

If you trust your adult children make them part of the process. Don't be afraid to tell the insurance company or the independent agent you're working with that you need some additional time to think before making a decision.

CHAPTER THIRTEEN

PLANNING THE MEDICARE BUYING DECISION

Now that we have covered the various Medicare programs in detail, you must now decide how you're going to get your Medicare health coverage. As a starting point you can get your health care coverage by enrolling in either original Medicare or in a Medicare Advantage plan.

If you go with original Medicare you may want to add at least a Medicare Prescription Drug Part D plan and/or a Medicare Supplement/Medigap plan to cover those expenses which original Medicare doesn't. If you go with a Medicare Advantage plan a prescription drug plan is <u>usually</u> included in the plan.

The flowchart on the next page diagrams this process.

Figure 13.1 Medicare Coverage Flowchart

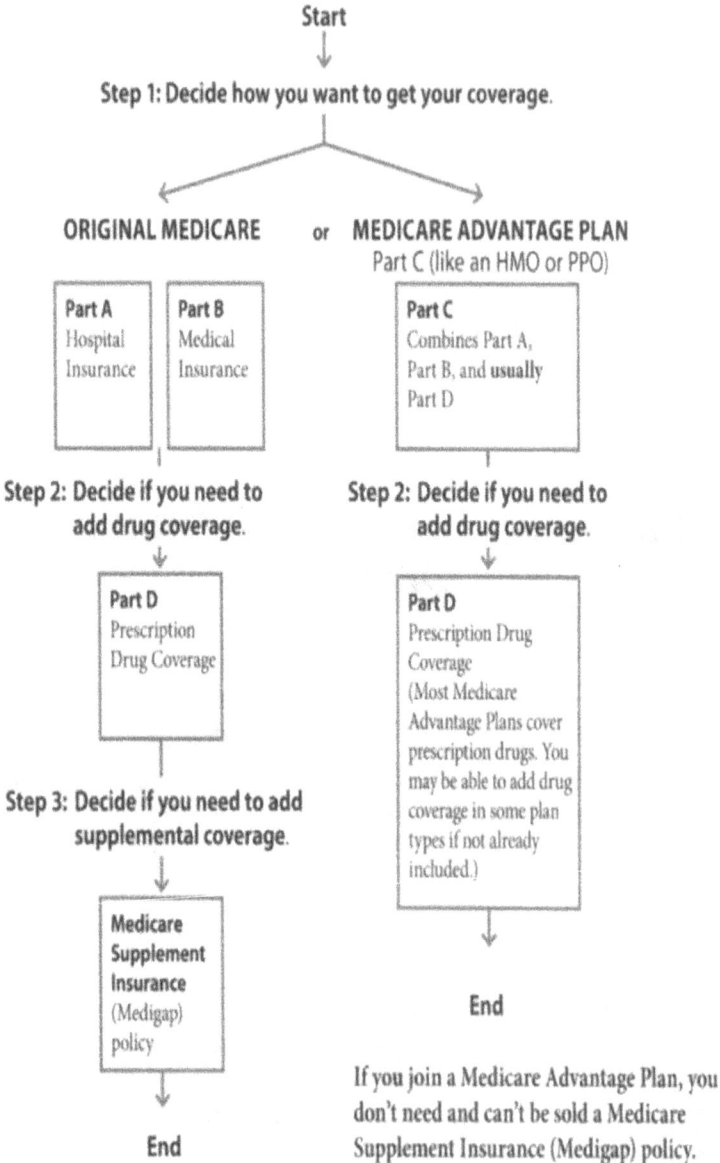

Start

Step 1: Decide how you want to get your coverage.

ORIGINAL MEDICARE or **MEDICARE ADVANTAGE PLAN**
Part C (like an HMO or PPO)

Part A	Part B
Hospital Insurance	Medical Insurance

Part C
Combines Part A, Part B, and usually Part D

Step 2: Decide if you need to add drug coverage.

Step 2: Decide if you need to add drug coverage.

Part D
Prescription Drug Coverage

Part D
Prescription Drug Coverage
(Most Medicare Advantage Plans cover prescription drugs. You may be able to add drug coverage in some plan types if not already included.)

Step 3: Decide if you need to add supplemental coverage.

Medicare Supplement Insurance
(Medigap) policy

End

End

If you join a Medicare Advantage Plan, you don't need and can't be sold a Medicare Supplement Insurance (Medigap) policy.

Courtesy: Centers for Medicare & Medicaid Services

236

Now let's take the same format as above and add some depth for a further understanding.

Figure 13.2 Medicare Coverage Flowchart Detail

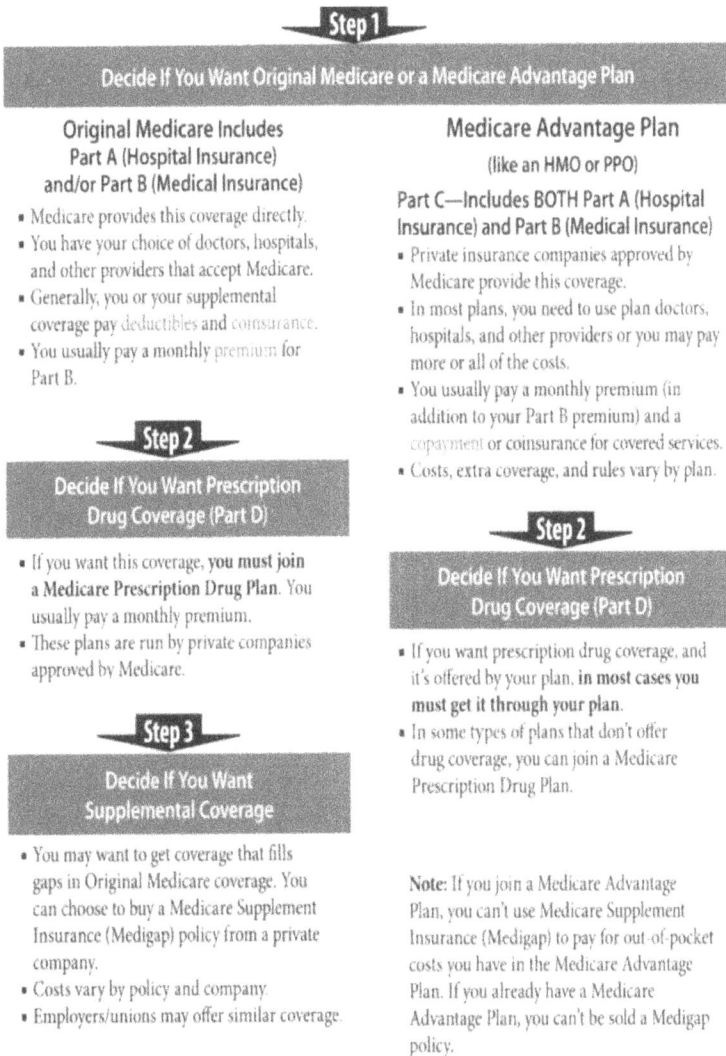

Step 1

Decide If You Want Original Medicare or a Medicare Advantage Plan

Original Medicare Includes
Part A (Hospital Insurance)
and/or Part B (Medical Insurance)

- Medicare provides this coverage directly.
- You have your choice of doctors, hospitals, and other providers that accept Medicare.
- Generally, you or your supplemental coverage pay deductibles and coinsurance.
- You usually pay a monthly premium for Part B.

Step 2

Decide If You Want Prescription Drug Coverage (Part D)

- If you want this coverage, **you must join a Medicare Prescription Drug Plan.** You usually pay a monthly premium.
- These plans are run by private companies approved by Medicare.

Step 3

Decide If You Want Supplemental Coverage

- You may want to get coverage that fills gaps in Original Medicare coverage. You can choose to buy a Medicare Supplement Insurance (Medigap) policy from a private company.
- Costs vary by policy and company.
- Employers/unions may offer similar coverage.

Medicare Advantage Plan
(like an HMO or PPO)

Part C—Includes BOTH Part A (Hospital Insurance) and Part B (Medical Insurance)

- Private insurance companies approved by Medicare provide this coverage.
- In most plans, you need to use plan doctors, hospitals, and other providers or you may pay more or all of the costs.
- You usually pay a monthly premium (in addition to your Part B premium) and a copayment or coinsurance for covered services.
- Costs, extra coverage, and rules vary by plan.

Step 2

Decide If You Want Prescription Drug Coverage (Part D)

- If you want prescription drug coverage, and it's offered by your plan, **in most cases you must get it through your plan.**
- In some types of plans that don't offer drug coverage, you can join a Medicare Prescription Drug Plan.

Note: If you join a Medicare Advantage Plan, you can't use Medicare Supplement Insurance (Medigap) to pay for out-of-pocket costs you have in the Medicare Advantage Plan. If you already have a Medicare Advantage Plan, you can't be sold a Medigap policy.

Courtesy: Centers for Medicare & Medicaid Services

WHERE TO BEGIN NOW

If you've read this entire book up to this point you have acquired the knowledge which puts you ahead of probably 95% of the individuals age 65 and older – congratulations. Where do you begin? You can start this process in any of a number of ways.

- By calling a number of insurance companies, which sell Medicare health plans to determine which plans are offered in the area where you live.
- Go on the internet and begin searching various insurance companies, which sell Medicare health plans to determine which plans are offered in the area where you live.
- Go to workshops in your area, which can be sponsored by the Medicare health insurance providers or independent insurance companies which sell their specific plans.
- Ask a friend or relative which type of plan they have, if they like it and how long they have been enrolled in the plan.
- Do it yourself online through the Medicare website at www.medicare.gov.

DO IT YOURSELF ROUTE

For those of you who are the Home Depot types and want to do everything yourself you can follow these guidelines. The steps which follow only apply if you are interested in a Medicare Advantage Part C plan or a Medicare Prescription Part D Drug plan. You cannot find Medicare Supplement plans using this particular process.

1. Make a list of the physicians you use, the hospitals or outpatient facilities you go to, your medical procedures done and the prescription drugs you take along with the dosage, how often you take them and how often you get them refilled. Don't include over-the-counter medication as these are not covered by Medicare.

2. Go to the Medicare.gov website and click the yellow button on the left, near the middle of the page which says "Find health & drug plans". If you haven't applied for Medicare yet there is another yellow button right next to it which will allow you to apply online. This takes you to the *Medicare Plan Finder* page. This tool will allow you to search for both Medicare Advantage and Prescription Drug plans in your service area.

3. Enter your zip code then click on the *"Find Plans"* brown button. Next, answer the two questions and the click the brown button "Continue to Plan Results."

4. Next enter the names of any prescription drug medications you are taking. This is a really easy to use tool. You can create a drug list with up to 25 of your prescription drugs. You can also easily print this list. If you want to skip the drug component for now; select either the *"I don't take any drugs"* or *"I don't want to add drugs now"* white buttons. If you skip this step Plan Finder will display prices that include estimated costs for all plans based on national averages that may

or may not be close to what you will actually pay. Click your response.

5. You will then see a *"Summary of Your Search Results"*. It will indicate the number of plans in your service area including original Medicare. These results will be for 2014 plan data. This will list the number of plans available in your service area by three categories:

- Prescription Drug Plans (with original Medicare)
- Medicare Health Plans with drug coverage
- Medicare Health Plans without drug coverage

Next, if you like, you can "Refine Your Search" with a number of updates listed to the left. Otherwise click the *"Continue To Plan Results"* brown button.

6. You will see a display of *"Your Plan Results"*. After the original Medicare plan data you will see the available plans in your service area. One note, this view defaults to show only 10 plans. Depending on the number of plans that are displayed just below the category name you will see three buttons you can select; "View 10", "View 20", "View 50". They will display all the plans.

This tool is excellent to use and is very user friendly. It will definitely save you a lot of research time. As with anything, the more you use it the easier it will be become. You'll be a master navigator in no time at all.

YOU WANT HELP ENROLLING

As was indicated earlier, Medicare Advantage plans and Medicare Prescription Part D Drug plans must be purchased from a private insurance company which are approved by and contracted with Medicare. This means you will be dealing with a licensed insurance agent, either face-to-face or over the telephone who is either an employee of the insurance company or is an independent licensed insurance agent who is appointed with that insurance company. The insurance company must obtain approval of their paper, electronic (internet or facsimile) and telephone processes ahead of each annual enrollment season. Agents must use CMS approved tools. Most enrollment processes are similar. Below are some of the steps you'll probably encounter when purchasing and enrolling for a Medicare Advantage plan.

Statement of Understanding (SOU)

This document is required whether you enroll via paper, electronic or by telephone. When you sign the Medicare Advantage and/or Medicare Part D Enrollment application you are acknowledging your understanding of many disclosure items. The SOU can vary between different types of plans. Listed below are some of the items which you will acknowledge on the Statement of Understanding.

- Requirement to keep Medicare Part A and B.
- Agrees to follow plan rules.
- Enrollment is generally for one year.
- Late enrollment penalties exist.

- Date coverage begins.
- Right to appeal service and payment denials by the Plan.
- You may be enrolled in one Medicare Advantage and/or Part D plan. Enrollment into another Medicare Advantage and/or Part D plan will automatically disenroll you from any other MA or Part D plan.
- The MA plan has a contract with the federal government.
- Plan covers service area. If you move you must notify the plan.
- Fraud warnings – if you submit, with intent, false information you have committed fraud which could result in disenrollment and be subject to civil or criminal liability.
- Importance of your signature.

Who May Complete Enrollment Application?

Generally, only the Medicare eligible individual may execute a valid enrollment or disenrollment request. However, a Durable Power of Attorney (DPOA) or authorized legal representative may execute the request on the individual's behalf.

You must complete an enrollment request to enroll in a Medicare Advantage plan during a valid enrollment period. If you are already a member in an MA plan and you wish to elect another MA plan offered by the **same** Medicare Advantage plan organization a short enrollment form maybe used in place of the individual Enrollment Application. Most enrollment types contain the same standard language except for a PFFS or MSA plan. Once the Plan receives an enrollment request, it must provide the individual with a notice of acknowledgement, denial or request for additional information within 10 days.

Non-Discrimination Requirements

Medicare Advantage plan sponsors are not allowed to discriminate on race, ethnicity, national origin, religion, gender, age, mental or physical disability, health status, claims experience, medical history and genetic information, evidence of insurability or geographic location within the service area. You may not be treated differently because of the above factors.

Every insurance company or agent that works with or is contracted with Medicare must obey the law. All items and services of an agent must be made available to all eligible individuals within the service area with the following exceptions.

- Some specific products and services may be made available to individuals with certain diagnoses.
- Enrollment in the LIS; as there may be additional eligibility requirements.

Plan Sponsor and Agent Requirements

The plan sponsor and agent are required to provide you with specific items prior to the enrollment effective date.

- Provide you a confirmation number at the time of enrollment if the enrollment is sent electronically.

- Send an acknowledgement letter confirming receipt of the Enrollment Application and showing the effective date within 10 calendar days after receipt of enrollment requests by the plan.
- Provide a copy of the Enrollment Application prior to the enrollment effective date or within 10 calendar days of the Enrollment Application completion date, whichever occurs first.
- Proof of health insurance coverage so you may begin using plan services as of the effective date.

After Enrolling in a Medicare Advantage or Medicare Prescription Drug Plan

After you have completed the enrollment application and it has been submitted, for either a Medicare Advantage or Medicare Prescription Part D Drug plan the following will happen. CMS requires all plan sponsors to complete an "outbound enrollment and verification (OEV)" call to the applicant within 15 days of receiving your enrollment application. Usually the insurance companies will contract with a third-party firm to make these calls. The purpose of the call is to ensure the Medicare Advantage or Medicare Prescription Drug plan was clearly and thoroughly explained to you. The customer service representatives are typically not licensed so they cannot answer any questions about the plan. The survey is usually less than 15 questions long. They will also explain the 7-day cancellation language which is required by Medicare.

FINAL THOUGHTS

At the end of the day <u>you</u> must make the decision. Each program and plan has its pros and cons. The key decisions usually come down to health, coverage and money. As I tell individuals many times, the automotive company FRAM, use to run commercials (http://www.youtube.com/watch?v=aq3wL8ZXjBU) which had this marketing slogan at the end of the commercials which was, *"The choice is yours. You can pay me now or pay me later."* While this is a generalized analogy in health care it has some merit here.

With a Medicare Supplement/Medigap plan there is a monthly premium you pay every month (*pay me now*) whether to go to a physician or not. When you need medical services most if not all costs will be covered, depending on the letter of the Med Supp plan you have, and the medical bill for services rendered will be sent directly to the health insurance company. There's nothing more for you to do.

With many Medicare Advantage plans available today there are plans with $0 premiums each month, so there is no monthly premium cost to you now. However, if you need to see a physician or have a medical procedure done there are copays and coinsurance which you will be responsible for (*pay me later*).

With Medicare health plans it certainly is a case of the choice is yours. You can pay for care now or pay for care later.

"It seems as though there are Members in this body who want to filibuster just about everything we try to do, whether it is stopping judicial nominations, the Energy bill, or this Medicare bill."

Jim Bunning
Former Republican U.S. Senator - Kentucky
Republican U.S. House of Representatives –
Kentucky's 4th Congressional District
Former Major League Baseball Pitcher

CHAPTER FOURTEEN

ADDITIONAL MEDICARE RESOURCES

If you have questions about Medicare, Social Security, Railroad Retirement, Medicaid, Veterans Affairs, Long Term Care resources or need updated phone numbers for the contacts listed, you can do the following:

1. Visit www.medicare.gov:

- For Medigap policies in your area visit www.medicare.gov/medigap.
- For updated phone numbers visit www.medicare.gov/contacts.

2. Call 1-800-MEDICARE (1-800-633-4227):

- For general or claims-specific information customer service representatives are available

24 hours a day, 7 days a week. TTY users should call 1-877-486-2048. You can get information 24 hours a day, including weekends. If you need help in a language other than English or Spanish let the customer service representative know the language.

3. Social Security (1-800-772-1213)

- Get a replacement Medicare card.
- Change your name or address.
- Eligibility, entitlement and enrollment information for Part A and/or Part B.
- Apply for Extra Help with prescription costs.
- TTY users should call 1-800-325-0778.
- Visit www.socialsecurity.gov.

4. Coordination of Benefits Contractor

- Find out if Medicare or your other insurance pays first and to report changes in your insurance information.
- Call 1-800-999-1118.
- TTY users should call 1-800-318-8782.

5. Department of Defense

- Information about the TRICARE for Life (TFL) and the TRICARE Pharmacy program.
- TFL call 1-866-773-0404.
- TTY users should call 1-866-773-0405.
- Pharmacy call 1-877-363-1303.
- TTY users should call 1-877-540-6261.
- Visit www.tricare.mil/mybenefit.

6. Department of Health and Human Services – Office for Civil Rights

- Think you were discriminated against or if your health information privacy rights were violated.
- Call 1-800-368-1019.
- TTY users should call 1-800-537-7697.
- Visit www.hhs.gov/ocr.

7. Department of Veterans Affairs

- You're a veteran or have served in the U.S. military.
- Call 1-800-829-4833.
- TTY users should call 1-800-829-4833.
- Visit www.va.gov.

8. Office of Personnel Management

- Information about the Federal Employee Health Benefits Program for current and retired Federal employees.
- Call 1-888-767-6738.
- TTY users should call 1-800-878-5707.
- Visit www.opm.gov/insure.

9. Railroad Retirement Board (RRB)

- Receiving benefits from the RRB.
- Call 1-877-772-5772.
- Visit www.rrb.gov.

10. Below are some additional telephone numbers that may be useful.

- Senior Medicare Patrol: 877-808-2468 to find out location of nearest office.
- Medicare Fraud Hotline: 800-447-8477 if you suspect fraud.
- Do Not Call Registry: 888-382-1222.

11. Resources for Long-Term Care

- The *National Clearinghouse for Long-Term Care Information* website, www.longtermcare.gov. The *U.S. Department of Health and Human Services* developed this website to provide information and resources to help you and your family plan for future long-term care (LTC) needs.
- To find out about in-law apartments visit the *National Resource Center on Supportive Housing and Home Modification* website, www.gero.usc.edu/nrcshhm.
- Visit the *U.S. Department of Housing and Urban Development-Persons with Disabilities* section 811, www.hud.gov, to find subsidized housing for persons with disabilities.
- The local community Area Agency on Aging can be found by visiting the *Eldercare Locator* website, http://www.eldercare.gov, or calling 1-800-677-1116 to obtain information about available services in your area. You may also find more information about board and care facilities in your area from the *Administration on Aging (AoA)* website, www.aoa.gov.
- You may also find more information about assisted living facilities in your area from the *Administration on Aging (AoA)* website. You can

also contact the *Assisted Living Federation of America (ALFA)*, www.alfa.org and the *National Center for Assisted Living (NCAL)*, www.ahcancal.org.

- You can find out if a CCRC is accredited and get advice on selecting this type of long-term care community from the *Commission on Accreditation of Rehabilitation Facilities*, www.carf.org/home. You can also get more information about continuing care retirement communities from the *Administration on Aging (AoA)* and the *American Association of Homes and Services for the Aging (AAHSA)*, www.healthfinder.gov.
- To find out information on accreditation of nursing homes in your area, look at the *Joint Commission on the Accreditation of Healthcare Organizations' (JCAHO)* website, www.jointcommission.org.

12. State Health Insurance Assistance Program

SHIPs are state programs which get their money from the Federal government to give local health insurance counseling to people with Medicare. Services include:

- Get free personalized Medicare counseling on decisions about coverage.
- Help with claims, billing or appeals.
- Information on programs for individuals with limited income and resources.

Table 14.1 State Health and Insurance Departments

State	State Health Insurance Program	State Insurance Department
Alabama	1-800-243-5463	1-800-433-3966
Alaska	1-800-478-6065	1-800-467-8725
American Samoa	Not Available	1-684-633-4116
Arizona	1-800-432-4040	1-800-325-2548
Arkansas	1-800-224-6330	1-800-224-6330
California	1-800-434-0222	1-800-927-4357
Colorado	1-888-696-7213	1-800-930-3745
Connecticut	1-800-994-9422	1-800-203-3447
Delaware	1-800-336-9500	1-800-282-8611
Florida	1-800-963-5337	1-877-693-5236
Georgia	1-800-669-8387	1-800-656-2298
Guam	1-671-735-7388	1-671-635-1835
Hawaii	1-888-875-9229	1-808-586-2790
Idaho	1-800-247-4422	1-800-721-3272
Illinois	1-800-548-9034	1-866-445-5364
Indiana	1-800-452-4800	1-800-622-4461
Iowa	1-800-351-4664	1-877-955-1212
Kansas	1-800-860-5260	1-800-432-2484
Kentucky	1-877-293-7447	1-800-595-6053
Louisiana	1-800-259-5301	1-800-259-5300
Maine	1-877-353-3771	1-800-300-5000
Maryland	1-800-243-3425	1-800-492-6116
Massachusetts	1-800-243-4636	1-617-521-7794
Michigan	1-800-803-7174	1-877-999-6442
Minnesota	1-800-333-2433	1-800-657-3602
Mississippi	1-800-948-3090	1-800-562-2957
Missouri	1-800-390-3330	1-800-726-7390
Montana	1-800-551-3191	1-800-332-6148
Nebraska	1-800-234-7119	1-800-234-7119

State	State Health Insurance Assistance Program	State Insurance Department
Nevada	1-800-307-4444	1-800-992-0900
New Hampshire	1-866-634-9412	1-800-852-3416
New Jersey	1-800-792-8820	1-800-446-7467
New Mexico	1-800-432-2080	1-800-947-4722
New York	1-800-701-0501	1-800-342-3736
North Carolina	1-800-443-9354	1-800-546-5664
North Dakota	1-800-247-0560	1-800-247-0560
Northern Mariana Islands	Not Available	1-670-664-3064
Ohio	1-800-686-1578	1-800-686-1526
Oklahoma	1-800-763-2828	1-800-522-0071
Oregon	1-800-722-4134	1-888-877-4894
Pennsylvania	1-800-783-7067	1-877-881-6388
Puerto Rico	1-877-725-4300	1-888-722-8686
Rhode Island	1-401-462-0530	1-401-462-9520
South Carolina	1-800-868-9095	1-803-737-6160
South Dakota	1-877-331-4834	1-605-773-3563
Tennessee	1-877-801-0044	1-800-342-4029
Texas	1-800-252-9240	1-800-252-3439
Utah	1-877-424-4640	1-800-439-3805
Vermont	1-800-642-5119	1-800-631-7788
Virgin Islands St. Thomas	1-340-772-7368 1-340-714-4354	1-340-774-7166
Virginia	1-800-552-3402	1-877-310-6560
Washington	1-800-562-6900	1-800-562-6900
Washington D.C.	1-202-994-6272	1-202-727-8000
West Virginia	1-877-987-4463	1-888-879-9842
Wisconsin	1-800-242-1060	1-800-236-8517
Wyoming	1-800-856-4398	1-800-438-5768

Source: Centers for Medicare & Medicaid Services

"We're saying no changes for Medicare for people above the age of 55. And in order to keep the promise to current seniors who've already retired and organized their lives around this program, you have to reform it for the next generation."

Paul Ryan
Republican U.S. House of Representatives –
Wisconsin's 1st Congressional District
2012 Republican Vice-Presidential Running Mate

About the Author

Stephen J. Stellhorn is the founder of MSM Capital Management, LLC (MSM). His financial services career spans over twenty-five years in banking, investments and insurance. He has held positions in retail and institutional bond sales, fixed income portfolio management, U.S. Government bond trading, bank balance sheet management, brokerage branch sales management and insurance and financial planning.

The retirement model in the 21st century will be designed by collaborating with clients to assist them in developing a blueprint for understanding and efficiently utilizing their personal capital. When optimized, these capital sources; human, social and financial work synergistically to create a floor of income to offset "essential" expenses no matter what market conditions exist. This holistic approach to longevity planning is vastly different from traditional investment and retirement planning.

MSM's focus is personal capital management. Working together with clients, an assessment of their personal capital is established. From there, a plan is created for retirement income sustainability. This plan integrates both health care and social security planning. This approach ensures clients have an objective and unbiased assessment of where they are at and what action steps may need to be taken. As a solutions integrator, MSM provides Medicare health plans, health, dental, life, long-term care and final expense insurance along with annuities. For further information, visit www.msmcapital.net.

Stellhorn holds the Retirement Management Analyst (RMA℠) designation through the Retirement Income Industry Association® (RIIA®), of which he is an individual member. He has passed the FINRA securities exams for the Series 7, 8, 24, 4, 27, 55, 63 and 65, and also the MSRB securities exams for the Series 52 and 53. Stellhorn has also passed the State of Florida 2-15 insurance exam. He is a Florida licensed insurance agent, appointed with a number of insurance carriers.

He has also completed the Retirement Management Analyst Program at Boston University's Center for Professional Education. He completed and received a Certificate in Financial Planning from Kaplan University. He is a graduate of The Florida State University; earning dual Bachelor of Science degrees in International Business and Biological Science. Stellhorn is a member of the fraternity of Phi Gamma Delta.

Past firms he has been associated with include Waddell & Reed Financial Advisors, AXA Advisors, LLC, Charles Schwab & Co., ABN AMRO North America, European American Bank (EAB), NCNB, Pan American Bank, Mabon Nugent & Co. and Southeast Bank.

He resides in Tampa, Florida with his lovely wife Linda, three boomeranging college students and his beloved Shih Tzu - Jagger.

256

Index

A

ACA, *215*
Accelerated death benefits, 194
Administration on Aging, *250*
Affordable Care Act, *39*
American Association for Long-
    Term Care Insurance, *169*,
    205
American Association of Homes
    and Services for the Aging,
    251
ANOC
    annual letter, *49*
Assignment, *50*
Attained-age rated, *155*

B

Balanced Budget Act 1997, *105*
Barker, Bob, *104*
Benefit period, *50*
Bertolini, Mark, *14*
Born to Run, ix
Bunning, Jim, *246*
Bureau of Labor Statistics
    Consumer expenditure survey,
    14

C

Centers for Disease Control and
    Prevention, *123*
Chart
    Angiogram imaging cost, *9*
    Average annual health care
        premiums, *6*
    Cataract surgery cost, *11*
    Characteristics of the Medicare
        population, *30*
    Colonoscopy cost, *12*
    Comparision of Medigap plans,
        146
    Complaints by enrollee, *231*
    Coronary atery bypass surgery
        cost, *10*
    Cost per hospital day, *8*
    Cumulative increases in health
        insurance premiums, *5*
    Cymbalta drug cost, *12*
    Demand curves, *15*
    Donut hole, *130*
    Estimated health care costs, *xv*
    Future makeup of GDP, *4*
    Health care spending, *2*
    Hip replacement cost, *11*
    Lipitor drug cost, *13*
    Median per capita incomes, *25*
    Median per capita savings, *26*
    Medicare beneficiaries as a
        percentage, *24*

Medicare coverage flowchart, *236*
Medicare enrollment, *23*
MRI imaging cost, *10*
Nexium drug cost, *13*
Obtaining health care post 65, *29*
Popoulation 65+, *4*
Routine office visit cost, *9*
Chronic illness rider, *195*
CMS, *22*, *27*
Consistent Poor Performer Notice, *40*
Illegal agent sales practices, *231*
National Health Expenditures Projections 2011-2021, *1*
Sales practice rules, *230*
Star rating measurements, *39*
Star rating system, *37*
Coinsurance, *50*
Commission on Accreditation of Rehabilitation Facilities, *251*
Community-no age rated, *154*
Copayment, *50*
Creditable prescription drug coverage, *51*
Critical access hospital, *51*
Custodial care, *51*

D

Daltrey, Roger, *x*
Deductible, *51*
Dent, Harry S.
Demand curves, *15*
Department of Defense, *248*
Department of Health and Human Service, *170*
Department of Housing and Urban Development-Persons with Disabilities, 250
Department of Veterans Affairs, *249*

E

Eldercare locator, *250*
Entwistle, John, *x*
Excess charge, *51*
Express Scripts, *75*
Extra Help, *51*

F

Fidelity Benefits Consulting, *xv*
Figure 11.1
Agent bonus, *230*
Formulary, *52*

G

Guaranteed issue rights, *52*
Guaranteed renewable policy, *52*

H

Hayworth, Nan, *162*
Health Affairs, *14*
Health and Human Services, *22*
Health and Human Services – Office for Civil Rights, *249*
Health Insurance Marketplaces, *22*, *43*

I

Indemnity Policy, *185*
Inpatient rehabilitation facility, *52*
Integrated Policy, *185*
International Federation of Health Plans, *7*
Issue-age rated, *154*

J

Johnson, Lyndon B., *78*
Joint Commission on the Accreditation of Healthcare Organization, *251*

K

Kaiser Family Foundation, *135*

L

Licensed insurance agents, *228*
Life Insurance and Market Research Association, *169*
Life settlements, *198*
Lifetime reserve days, *52*
Long-Term Care
Assisted living, *178*
Board and care homes, *177*
Community-based services, *176*
Comparison of LTC types and assistance offered, *175*
Continuing care retirement communities, *178*
Determining insurance rates, *182*
Filial support laws, *209*
Home health care, *176*
Housing for aging and disabled individuals, *177*
In-law apartments, *177*
Least costly states, *172*
LTCI benefits and eligibility, *186*
LTCI tax advantages, *188*
Most costly states, *172*
No prior experience, *166*
Nursing homes, *179*
Survey - Genworth Financial, *168, 170*
Survey - John Hancock, *164*
Survey - Nationwide Financial, *165*
Survey - Northwestern Mutual, *165*
Survey - U.S. Trust, *166*
Triggering an LTC event, *174*
Types of LTCI policies, *185*
Viatical benefits received based on life expectancy, *202*
Long-term care insurance rider, *196*

M

Medicaid
Affordable Care Act, *214*
Benefits, *219*
Created, *213*
Eligibility, *216*
Federal Poverty Level, *217*
Ineligibility period, *222*
Marketplace for Individuals, *215, 216*
Medical underwriting, *53*
Medically necessary, *53*
Medicare
2014 - What's new and important, *45*
Additional resources, *247*
COBRA, *61*
Created, *21*
Durable medical equipment, *86*
Enrollment period, *56*
General enrollment period, *60*
Group retiree, *35*
Inital enrollment period, *57*
Medicare health programs, *27*
Part A home health care, *85*
Part A hospice, *86*
Part A hospitalization, *80*
Part A inpatient hospital care, *81*
Part A long-term care hospitals, *82*
Part A premiums, *89*
Part A premiums entirely waived, *79*
Part A skilled nursing care, *85*

Part A skilled nursing facility, 82
Part B covered services, 99
Part B high income earners, 95
Part B medical insurance, 93
Part B non-covered services, 102
Part B premiums, 94
Penalties for late enrollment, 62
Plan finder, 239
Planning the decision, 235
Special enrollment period, 61
Medicare Advantage
    Additional member benefits, 112
    Completing an enrollment, 242
    Covered benefits, 111
    Created, 105
    Florida, 115
    HMO, 107
    Medicare medical savings
        account, 109
    Medicare+Choice, 105
    Non-discrimination
        requirements, 243
    Outbound enrollment and
        verification call, 244
    PFFS, 109
    PPO, 108
    Premiums, 110
    SNP, 108
    Sponsor and agent requirements,
        243
    Statement of understanding, 241
    Switching plans, 113
    Types of plans, 107
Medicare Advantage Plans
    Annual enrollment period, 65
    Disenrollment, 71
    General enrollment period, 65
    Initial enrollment period, 63
    Special enrollment period, 66
Medicare Payment Advisory
    Commission, 31
Medicare Prescription Drug
    Plans
    General enrollment period, 68
    initial enrollment period, 67

Initial enrollment period, 67
Open enrollment period, 68
Penalties for late enrollment, 70
Special enrollment period, 69
Medicare Prescription Drug,
    Improvement, and
    Modernization Act of 2003,
    105
Medicare Prescription Drugs
    Coverage rules, 126
    Florida, 139
    Formularies and tiers, 133
    High income earners, 129
    Low income subsidy, 136
    MA-PD, 124
    PDP, 124
    Premium costs, 127
    Standard benefits, 125
    TrOOP, 129
Medicare Savings Program,
    90
Medicare Savings Programs,
    90
Medicare Summary Notice, 32
Medicare Supplement/Medigap,
    144
    Florida, 157
    Guaranteed issue rights, 147
    Massachusetts, 150
    Medicare SELECT, 146
    Minnesota, 151
    Premium costs, 153
    Pricing policies, 154
    Switching plans, 155
    Types of plans, 145
    Wisconsin, 152
Medicare Supplement/Medigap
    Plans
    Open enrollment period, 70
Medicare-approved amount, 53
MONEY magazine, 233
Moon, Keith, x
My Generation, x

N

National Association of Insurance Commissioners, *184*

National Clearinghouse for Long Term Care, *173*

National Clearinghouse for Long-Term Care Information, *250*

National Council on Aging, *40*

National Resource Center on Supportive Housing and Home Modification, *250*

Non-tax qualified, *188*

O

Office of Personnel Management, *249*

Oliver Wyman, *47*

P

PACE, *28*

Parago, Jewel, *vii*

Peale, Norman Vincent, *viii*

Physician referral, *54*

Pre-existing condition, *53*

Premium, *53*

Preventive services, *54*

Primary care physician, *54*

Q

Quality Improvement Organization, *54*

R

Railroad Retirement Board, *22, 249*

Reimbursement or Expense Incurred Policy, *185*

Romer, Christina, *1*

Ronald Regan, *230*

Rubio Marco, *226*

Ryan, Paul, *254*

S

Scott, Rick, *212*

Service area, *54*

Shimkus, John, *122*

Snowe, Olympia, *48*

Social Security, *57, 248*

Social Security Administration, *22*

Songfacts, *x*

Springsteen, Bruce, *ix*

State Children's Health Insurance Program, *22*

State Health Insurance Assistance Program (SHIP), *251*

Stellhorn, Stephen J., *255*

Sununu, John, *20*

T

Tax qualified, *188*

The Who, *x*

Townshend, Pete, *x*

TRICARE, *248*

U

University of Pittsburgh, *135*

V

Viatical settlements, *201*

www.ingramcontent.com/pod-product-compliance
Lightning Source LLC
Chambersburg PA
CBHW070800280326
41934CB00012B/2991